how to know

robert mchenry

How to Know

Copyright © 1998, 2004 by Robert McHenry

ISBN 1-59113-523-0

Printed in the United States of America.

Booklocker.com, Inc.
2004

how to know

table of contents

introduction

The so-called "Information Age" in which we are said to be living is notoriously a time of information explosion and overload. Ask anybody. On the other hand, it is only occasionally noticed that this Information Age has not automatically made us all smarter. More information does not mean more knowledge, less error, better judgments. Those real benefits come only with effort and skill – thinking, in other words, and thinking well. To the contrary, there is evidence that the flood of cheap information has encouraged credulity. Certainly the Internet has made possible the mass distribution of the most arrant nonsense, which seems to find a waiting and willing audience.

Whether it is actually true that individuals are in fact and in feeling overwhelmed by masses of information and the consequent need to sort out the good from the bad, the possibly true from the likely false, the constant talk of it has begun to call renewed attention to a very old problem: What do we reliably know? What can we reliably know? How ought we to regard the many claims to knowledge that we confront, and would like to make, daily?

The branch of philosophy known as epistemology has contended with these and deeper issues for millennia and has neither solved them nor provided much help with them for most people. The first failure (if that is what it is) is of consequence chiefly to the professional philosophers, but the second leaves a great and growing need for the rest of us. Whether or not we are sinking in a sea of information, it is surely the case that life is more complex than ever, that in our ordinary, non-philosophical ways we encounter claims and counterclaims constantly, and that we are called on to decide on the basis of what we think we know or what someone tells us they know.

In recent years the epistemologists have been joined by a growing corps of linguists, cognitive scientists, computer scientists, evolutionary biologists, and others in the attempt to understand the nature of human cognition. And while, again, their work is abstruse, highly technical, often incomprehensible to any but the anointed, many of their results bear on the general problem of knowing. *How to Know* attempts to integrate some particularly relevant results of the work of all these professionals into a discussion that is accessible to the layman. The aim is not to popularize the philosophy, the cognitive science, the evolutionary science – there are already a number of excellent books that do those jobs, and the flow shows no sign of abating. Rather, the aim is to use some of that work to illuminate a reexamination of the old, old problem, How sure can I be that I know what I know? It is, then, a book about the practical business of what we think of as "knowing" in everyday life. It is about what we mean, or can mean, when we say "I know that [something or other]," and it is about how we may go about forming judgments when other people offer statements of that kind.

It is worthwhile to notice this early on the traditional distinction between knowing *that* and knowing *how*. I may know *that*, for example, the standard typing keyboard employs what is called the QWERTY arrangement of letters, from the first row of keys for the left hand, and that this arrangement has persisted virtually unchanged since the introduction of the first commercial Remington model in 1874, despite the later development of demonstrably superior layouts. But this does not mean that I know *how* to type. The reverse is also true. Flirting with paradox, we may say that this book concerns itself with Knowing How to Know That (though I decided in the end that would make a poor title).

We all often hear, and perhaps sometimes use, phrases like "right to know" and "need to know." What is it, exactly, that is being asserted in such phrases? Presumably it has something to do with being correctly informed about something. How do I know whether I am or am not in that state? If I have a right to vote, I know what circumstances and actions will constitute fulfillment of that right: At a time and place made known to all, I will present credentials attesting my right and be given access to a ballot or a voting booth (or perhaps a set of colored marbles); I will make a choice and indicate it in the manner provided; and, finally and critically, my vote will be counted in among those of all others who have exercised their right to vote. How am I to know, though, when my "right to know" has been satisfied? Likewise, when I claim a need to eat, the nature of that claim and the reality underlying it are plain to all. Is the "need to know" anything like that? What counts as knowing, and who counts it?

How to Know considers the question of how we come to believe that we know things. What is this stuff we call knowledge, and where does it come from? How far can we trust it? If it is less than entirely reliable, what then? Most important, it argues that knowledge doesn't just happen, but that each of us is actively involved in its construction and that we can do the work well or not well but will have to take responsibility for the outcome in either case. *How to Know* does not offer training in logic or analysis or research; rather, it attempts to insert a foundation beneath the specific mental skills and to bring the reader to an understanding of how and why those skills work, and how and why they don't.

So this is not a book about epistemology. I am not an epistemologist. Real epistemologists may not agree about much, but they will readily agree that the next book in their field should not be written by me. Yet my interest in these questions will not seem odd, I think, given my more than thirty years in the business of reference publishing. I have used, written, and edited books that exist for the purpose of permitting that which one person knows to be transmitted to another person who wishes to know it, and in the process I have come to *know* a little something about that transaction.

As befits so enormous a subject, this is a small book. I have always myself been drawn to small books, and not merely because I am a slow reader. Small books suggest that the author has given enough thought to the matter at hand to have arrived at a clear view of it that can be expressed economically. They suggest that the author has sufficient respect for both the matter and his audience to strive to convey the former straightforwardly, that the latter may get on with their real business.

1: tales of the unknown

> It ain't so much the things we don't know
> that get us into trouble. It's the things we do
> know that just ain't so.
> —Artemus Ward

It is perfectly legitimate for you to wonder what is meant by the title of this book. That effect is, of course, calculated. For my purpose, it is more important that you note what it is not called. It is not called What to Know. The choice of what to know, or rather the lifelong series of such choices, or more properly still the lifelong series of choices of what to seek to know, is yours and yours alone, though a good many people, not including me, will try to influence you in those choices. It is precisely because of that – because you will not be left alone to know or not to know as you will – that help is offered in the form of this book.

You may be thinking that you already know a great many things and, with the chastening experience of having made some minor mistakes along the way – quite small ones, really, were they not? – you may well feel that by now you have a nicely workable method in hand for knowing still more. If this is your view, you are overconfident and ought to read on. You may even take the view that knowing things is easy and getting them wrong from time to time matters little. If so, you are a harder case, but I hope to reach you as well. To do so I begin with a few cautionary tales. While each illustrates one or more violations of the rules of clear thinking, they are, more pointedly, examples of how serious the question of knowing or not knowing can be. They might collectively justify the title of "How Not to Know," or, less kindly, "How to Snatch Error from the Jaws of Knowledge." They by no means amount to a full

1

catalog either of mental missteps or simple human vanity. They do show clearly that this question of how to know, how to assess what we know, and how much confidence to place in what we think we know, is as old as civilization and has not been solved by practice, evolution, technology, or more civilization.

In the final chapter we will return to these four tales and attempt to extract some sort of useful lesson.

oh! ambiguity!

One of the most renowned figures of the ancient world was Croesus, whose name was to become synonymous with great wealth. For about 14 years in the middle of the 6th century BC he ruled Lydia, on the Anatolian coast, and he was successful in expanding the kingdom he had inherited from his father, Alyattes. He conquered most of Greek Anatolia, beginning with Ephesus and at length including all the Greek states of Ionia and Æolia. Conquest had its usual effect in whetting Croesus' appetite for yet more power and wealth. He then turned on and overpowered other peoples of Anatolia – Herodotus catalogues the tribes under his rule as the "Lydians, Phrygians, Mysians, Nariandynians, Chalybians, Paphlagonians, Thynian and Bithynian Thracians, Carians, Ionians, Dorians, Æolians and Pamphylians."

A famous story has Solon, the Athenian lawgiver, visiting Croesus and lecturing him on the transitory nature of earthly good fortune and the vanity of thinking oneself happy. The lecture did not please the king, to whom it seemed quite reasonable, in light of his vast wealth, to consider himself the happiest of men. The only blight of which he was aware was the fact that one of his two sons was deaf and mute, a fact

2

that made him dote upon the other, Atys, all the more. Perhaps in retribution for his effrontery in believing himself securely happy, some god or other sent a dream to Croesus in which he was warned that the favored son would die "by the blow of an iron weapon." Croesus took measures to prevent any such thing happening, forbidding the son to engage in battle and removing all weapons from the palace to safe places. In time, nonetheless, the prophecy of the dream came true. Atys was killed accidentally during a boar hunt by a trusted guest, and Croesus took the lesson and gave himself up to mourning for a period of two years.

At the end of that time Croesus was roused by anxiety over the growing power of the Persian empire to the east. Cyrus II (known as "the Great"), founder of the Achaemenian dynasty, had consolidated his hold on the Iranian tribes and then turned his eyes westward. Croesus decided not to wait for Cyrus to attack but to strike first. Prudently, however, he sought counsel from the chief oracles of Greece and Libya. Not only that, he decided to test the oracles to see which would give the truest answer to his question.

Messengers were sent to all the oracles with instructions to wait until a certain time on a certain day and then to ask what the king was doing at that moment. Croesus took care not to plan what he would be doing, instead waiting until almost the appointed hour and then thinking up the most unlikely action he could imagine: Taking a tortoise and a lamb, he killed them, cut them up, and boiled the pieces in a brass cauldron. When the messengers returned with the written answers of the various oracles, only that of Delphi had the right answer. Croesus resolved then to submit all his important questions to Delphi and to trust in the answers he received. Just to be certain of his ground, he lavished gifts upon the oracle and the Delphians.

At length, as his preparations for war matured, he sent to Delphi with the key question: Should he go to war with the Persians? To which the oracle replied that if Croesus attacked the Persians he would destroy a great empire.

The answer pleased Croesus enormously. He launched his attack by invading Cappadocia. At Pteria the Lydians (with numerous allies) and the Persians fought inconclusively. Croesus returned to his capital, Sardis, to gather more forces, but Cyrus pursued, stormed the city, and captured Croesus. Thus in that year, 546 BC, a great empire was indeed destroyed – the Lydian Empire, Croesus' own.

utter nonscience

In 1832 a Virginia farmer by the name of Edmund Ruffin published a book called *An Essay on Calcareous Manures*, in which he described his experiments in improving the crop yield of his farm by the use of lime, fertilizers, crop rotation, and other techniques. The book proved very popular and made Ruffin one of the most notable citizens of the South (so much so that thirty years later, then living in Charleston, South Carolina, he was given the honor of firing the first shot on Fort Sumter, beginning the American Civil War). Ruffin has nothing to do with this tale except to illustrate the state of agriculture before the modern era. There was a body of traditional practice – much of it just maxims, customs, or rules of thumb – that was the accumulation of centuries of experience with various crops in various climates and soils, and there were a few individuals who tried to systematize that practice in the hope of raising productivity. Understanding of why this or that practice worked or didn't, or worked in these conditions but not in others, lay in the future. Advances in chemistry and in

4

biology through the remainder of the 19th century would lay the groundwork, but real agricultural science was to be a 20th century achievement.

By the 1920s much had been accomplished. Perhaps the most exciting work was being done in the infant science of genetics. Some general principles of the heritability of characteristics in living things had been known from earliest times, and farmers had worked out rough guides for the breeding of livestock and selection of crops. But the work of Gregor Mendel, T.H. Morgan, and others began to reveal what was really going on behind the practice. A hypothesis that there are physical units in the organism that carry heritable characteristics gained experimental support from many sides. A debate over how change occurs in organisms – most specifically over the question of whether adaptive changes undergone by an individual can be transmitted to offspring, a view now mainly identified with the French naturalist Lamarck – was being won by those who held that heredity is exclusively governed by the hypothetical units, dubbed genes, which may from time to time undergo changes, or mutations, that cause offspring to differ in some specific way from parents. How and why such mutations occur was unknown, but it had been shown that they could be induced by, for example, exposure of the organism to ionizing radiation.

An understanding of how genes behave, assuming there were such things, promised to put the production of superior organisms, especially livestock and crop species, on a firm, predictable basis. In order for the agriculturists of any nation to make use of such knowledge, however, a certain level of economic, technical, and social development would be required. This level was absent from the Soviet Union, a political entity even younger than genetics. Until the 1930s agriculture there remained a feudal system of estates, serfs, and hidebound tradition, while the larger polity, under the dictatorships of Lenin and then of Stalin, gradually developed what we now recognize as the characteristics of a totalitarian state: arbitrary policies executed by a self-serving bureaucracy and enforced by terror.

From these circumstances emerged in the late 1920s one Trofim D. Lysenko, a minor worker in an agricultural test station. He had little knowledge of or patience with the requirements of science – testing, modification of hypotheses, more testing – but a native talent for self-promotion. Beginning with a technique called "vernalization," by which he claimed to have increased the yield of winter wheat, and with the help of sympathetic journalists, Lysenko commenced a meteoric rise to power. At a time when raising the productivity of Soviet agriculture was a desperate necessity, and when the nation similarly needed native heroes to prove the value of the Communist system, Lysenko was quickly taken up as the man of the hour, soon to become the man of the century. Under the circumstances, such facts as that "vernalization" was nothing new, had been tried many places for a century and had been found to be of little value, or that the greatly increased yields claimed by Lysenko were not verified to begin with and never later materialized, were ignored. Once endorsed by Stalin himself, Lysenko and his teachings were immune to criticism, and those who dared to doubt him found themselves out of work, imprisoned, exiled, or worse.

As part of his battle with critics and in order to create an institutional base for himself and to solidify Stalin's support, Lysenko developed the view that genetics was only a "pseudoscience," one created and promulgated by a capitalist society to justify its evil ways. In journal articles and in the popular press, Lysenko and his growing corps of allies – that role being the only available alternative to being his enemy – attached to genetics and to geneticists a variety of adjectives that, in arcane Soviet usage, were damning: "formalistic," "idealist," "reactionary," "metaphysical," "barren," "menshevizing." In place of this "bourgeois biology" they undertook to create an entirely separate biology, "agrobiology," that would be properly materialist, dialectical, Marxist.

By 1948 Lysenko ruled absolutely over the conduct of biological and agricultural research in the Soviet Union, and he held that power, little diminished, until 1964, by which time the bourgeois geneticists in the West had demonstrated the existence of the gene, had discovered its structure and mode of operation, and were beginning to decode its language. Lysenko's agrobiology, meanwhile, led to such "discoveries" as the transmutation of species (such as wheat into rye, cabbage into rutabaga, fir into pine) and the "law of species life," according to which individual organisms (such as sapling trees planted in a cluster) would decide to sacrifice themselves for the good of the species. These and other discoveries were arrived at by a kind of practical intuition, and the formal, time-consuming process of verification insisted upon by plodding bourgeois scientists was utterly disdained. When Lysenko's last protector, Khrushchev, fell from power, the Soviet Union rivaled the United States in space science but still was burdened by a backward, unproductive agricultural system.

the convenience of being ignorant

On December 8, 1941, the Congress of the United States of America, at the request of the President, declared war on the Empire of Japan. The immediate and precipitating cause of this action was the surprise attack by Japanese naval air forces on U.S. naval and military bases in Hawaii the day before, the date that would "live in infamy," according to the President.

As it happened, there was in Hawaii a substantial population of persons of Japanese birth or descent, and it was suspected long before it was generally known that some of them had engaged in intelligence activities on behalf of Japan. The success of the attack may have owed something to those activities. As it also happened, there was a substantial population of persons of Japanese birth or descent in California as well. Might some of them assist in an attack on or invasion of the mainland West Coast?

In the first days after Pearl Harbor such suspicions were muted. Newspapers and political and community leaders in California emphasized the need for calm and for the observance of law. Mob action, hasty conclusions about who might pose a danger, and even ordinary loose talk were discouraged. This generally restrained and responsible public attitude held for a time in the face of rumors and reports, later nearly all discredited, of sightings of Japanese ships or aircraft, of mysterious radio broadcasts from isolated spots along the coast, and even of landings of Japanese forces.

Gradually, however, the atmosphere changed. Many factors contributed to the change. In the wake of Pearl Harbor, Japanese forces in southern Asia and the western Pacific successfully attacked Malaya, Thailand, the Philippines, Guam, Wake Island, the Dutch East Indies, and elsewhere and began to seem invincible. The extent of the damage done to the U.S. Pacific Fleet at Pearl Harbor slowly sank in. Anti-Asian sentiment, long a feature of politics in California (it had originated as agitation against the Chinese, to whom the later-arriving and less numerous Japanese were at first favorably compared), began to reassert itself. Racist appeals in this case found hearers among some whose motivations were purely economic, chiefly farmers who resented the competition of more efficient Japanese or simply coveted their lands. Talk of the need to "do something" about the Japanese found its way from street corners into the newspapers and, inevitably, to politicians.

Meanwhile, the U.S. government had not failed to recognize what was at stake. In the long diplomatic runup to war both the military establishment and the Federal Bureau of Investigation had anticipated the possibility of espionage and perhaps even sabotage. In March 1941, nine months before Pearl Harbor, a clandestine raid on the Japanese consulate in Los Angeles, conducted by naval intelligence and the FBI, had discovered solid evidence of an espionage network operating up and down the West Coast. The raid effectively ended the threat. Known or suspected agents were thereafter tracked and their associates noted. Other sources of information were also exploited, with the result that by mid-1941 the intelligence agencies had compiled a list of something over 2,000 Japanese aliens who were considered to pose some degree of risk. All the agencies expressed confidence that the situation was well in hand and that no substantial danger existed of which they were unaware. Based on these prior investigations, in the 24 hours following the attack on Pearl Harbor the intelligence agencies, assisted by local police, took more than 700 Japanese aliens into custody, and two months later that number had risen to over 2,100.

But the ability of politicians and other interested parties to play upon the anxieties of the public easily overbore the assurances of the intelligence agencies, whose prudence could be made to seem rather a failure to exercise sufficient initiative. With the enlistment of members of the California congressional delegation, a movement to deal with all the Japanese – not merely those identified as potentially dangerous or those who were aliens but all, including the majority who were United States citizens even of second and third generation – quickly gathered momentum. For most who supported the movement, "deal with" meant "remove from their homes and intern somewhere in the interior."

For two months an increasingly heated debate was conducted within the federal government, among officials in the

Department of War, the Department of Justice, and the Army who shared in some degree responsibility for domestic security and the conduct of war. There were those who early on pressed for internment of the Japanese, and there were those who expressed constitutional scruples with respect to citizens and more generally those against whom no complaint could be lodged. In between were the many who simply wished to find a quick and sustainable solution to what was becoming a problem in public relations as well.

A central, though somewhat passive, figure in the debate was Lieutenant General John L. DeWitt, commanding general of the Fourth Army and of the Western Defense Command, headquartered in the Presidio in San Francisco. General DeWitt was a career Army man, though not a combat officer, and he was ill-prepared to deal with either the public-relations issues or the legal and political considerations that weighed heavily in Sacramento and Washington. He was clear on one point: He was determined not to suffer the fate of the Army and Navy commanders in Hawaii, both of whom had been found by official investigations and in the court of public opinion to have been negligent in failing to prevent, to detect, or at least to respond effectively to the Pearl Harbor attack.

The internal debate culminated in February 1942 in the decision to intern all Japanese, a decision formalized in an order signed on February 19 by President Franklin D. Roosevelt. A key document that laid the foundation for the decision was General DeWitt's "Final Recommendation," a memorandum submitted to the Secretary of War on February 14. (The memorandum was actually drafted by Karl Bendetsen, a lawyer and reserve Army officer then serving on the staff of the Provost Marshal General.) The "Final Recommendation" summarized the case for general internment of all those of Japanese descent and in doing so was forced to accommodate somehow the lack of any concrete evidence that the persons in question actually posed any danger to the war effort. The argument might have been built on such flimsy evidence as lay to hand, and it might have brought in mention of the earlier epionage ring and explicit reminders of the disaster at Pearl Harbor and perhaps even historical precedents for sabotage by alien populations. It might have used elaborate or subtle logic. It took neither of those approaches. Instead it distilled the argument into a single sentence of stunning simplicity. The sentence was this:

"The very fact that no sabotage has taken place to date is a disturbing and confirming indication that such action will be taken."

unlucky pierre

In 1996 Pierre Salinger was 71 years old and could look back with considerable satisfaction on a life of much accomplishment and ample material reward. Before the age of 20 he was in command of a Navy submarine chaser in the Pacific. He finished college after his World War II service and became a reporter. His gutsy investigations of jail conditions and the bail-bond system in California and of corruption in the Teamsters union brought him to the attention of Robert F. Kennedy and ultimately to the post of press secretary to the President of the United States. His work as liaison between the White House and the press during the years of Camelot and Cold War exposed him to international affairs at the highest level, while his much noted love of the good life kept him in touch with other men of the world in other walks. After leaving the press post he served for a few months as a U.S. senator, was involved in a large investment company, published a novel, and then resumed working as a journalist in Paris. By 1979 he was Paris bureau chief for ABC News. He covered the Iran hostage crisis closely and created an award-winning television documentary on the negotiations that finally won the release of the hostages. After leaving ABC in 1993 Salinger joined a prominent public-relations firm, and later still he became an independent public-relations consultant.

Pierre Salinger was clearly a man who had been around, who had seen the underside of things as well as the glitzy surface and knew the inner workings to boot. He was a man you'd love to have as a wise and indulgent uncle. He was a man you'd ask for advice about almost anything, and he was not a man you'd care to try to put one over on.

In July 1996 a Boeing 747 flying as TWA flight 800 exploded shortly after takeoff from Kennedy Airport in New York. The explosion tore the plane apart, and the debris fell over a large area of ocean south of Long Island; all 230 persons aboard were killed. The cause of the explosion remained a puzzle for many months while National Transportation Safety Board workers painstakingly recovered and pieced together the debris. In the end it was decided that a spark had ignited fuel fumes in an otherwise empty fuel tank. But initial speculation on the cause included the possibility of terrorist attack, either by a planted bomb or a missile, and even the possibility of "friendly fire" from some naval or military exercise. When a definitive explanation was slow in coming, suspicions were aroused in some circles that were inclined already to doubt anything asserted by official sources and to find evidence of conspiracy and coverup in any situation more complex than a game of solitaire.

In November, as the NTSB and the FBI continued to search the wreckage and other evidence for an answer, Pierre Salinger suddenly went on television in France to announce that he had been given documentary evidence supporting the friendly-fire hypothesis, evidence he described as constituting "very, very strong proof." The document had come to him, he said, from an agent of French intelligence, and he was more than a little taken aback when reporters told him that it appeared to be a version of one that had been proliferating on the Internet since August. Salinger's announcement made all the papers and the evening television news, but it was only a matter of days before he had been made to look like a dupe of the first water. Here is one version (of many) of the Internet-circulated document he had relied on:

Subject: TWA FLT 800 COVERUP

From: anonymous

Distribution: world

--(Anonymous source FBI)...REGARDING TWA FLT. 800--- Just got this from a friend (TWA accident) not a joke

I just received the following account of the downing of TWA Flight 800 and thought I would share it with you. I cannot vouch for the validity of the information, but will admit that it is interesting.

The message came to me from a man who was Safety Chairman for the Airline Pilots Association for many years and he is considered an expert on safety. He would not ever spead idle rumor. In short, he is usually quite certain before saying anything:

The following information about TWA Flight 800 was received this afternoon (6/22/96).

TWA Flight 800 was shot down by a U.S. Navy guided missile ship which was in area W-1-05. W-

105 is a Warning Area off the Southeast coast of Long Island is used by the military for missile firing and other military operations.

Guided missile ships travel all over the world defending the U.S. and they were conducting practice firings up over the top of a Navy P-3 radar plane who was on a Southwest heading about over the top of TWA 800. Evidently, the missile is supposed to go over the top of the P-3 and the accuracy of this missile is being measured by instrumentation in the P-3.

There was a USAir flight coming from the Southeast descending towards Providence, RI that had been cleared to 21,000 feet and the TWA 800 aircraft was restricted to 13,000 feet. The air traffic controller requested the USAir Flight to turn on his landing lights with the idea that TWA might see his lights and identify him. At that point, he would clear the TWA flight to continue his climb.

The P-3 was a non-beacon target (transponder OFF) flying southwest in the controlled airspace almost over TWA 800 and made NO calls to ATC. After the explosion, he continued is flight to the west and then called ATC and asked if they would like him to turn around and assist with the "accident"! You will remember that the first announcement about the accident came from the Pentagon. The spokesman mentioned that they were sending the Navy to the crash site. They immediately sent a Navy Captain who was replaced the next day by an Admiral. That admiral is still on the scene.

The FBI has conducted at least 3,000 eyewitness interviews and the NTSB has not been able to be a part of these interviews nor have any access to the contents of them. Some of those eyewitnesses reported seeing lights. Those were probably the landing lights of the USAir plane.

It has been a cover-up from the word go. The NTSB is there in name ONLY. All other announcements made by Mr. Bob Francis say absolutely nothing and notice that the FBI is always standing beside or behind Mr. Francis and its would appear that his job is to make sure that nothing is said ht would give ways "The Big Secret!"

It is time to end this farce and tell the public the real truth as to what happened to TWA 800. My source shall remain my own but the above information is true and I believe it will all become known soon. Now that all of you know the real truth.

words

"I *think* I can. I *think* I can. I *think* I can. I
thought I could. I *thought* I could. I *thought* I
could."
—Watty Piper [emphasis added]

As a kind of limbering-up exercise, may we take a moment to
savor the ambiguity of the title of this chapter? What do you
take it to mean? On paper, it's hard to know what meaning is
intended, though if I were to speak it to you, you would grasp
it immediately. If, for example, I gave each word almost equal
stress and spoke "words" at a pitch the same as or just slightly
lower than "knowing," you would infer that I am talking about
the act or state of being familiar with words. If, on the other
hand, I gave distinctly heavier stress to "knowing" and let
"words" drop to a much lower pitch, you might be a little
puzzled as to what I have in mind but you might guess that I
am thinking about words that have to do with knowing. It is
the latter that I mean to convey. We need not pursue this line
of thought further here. But if we consider pitch and stress as
elements of the information conveyed by the title phrase, we
may begin to appreciate how wide the gap may be between
simple information and knowledge.

By "knowing words," then, I mean those words – those verbs –
that we commonly use to mean that we have some form or
degree of knowledge about some matter. There are many such
verbs in English, and many, many shades of meaning made
possible by them. Preeminently, of course, there is simply
know. We say "I know that it is Tuesday." "I know that water
is composed of oxygen and hydrogen." "I know that Elvis is
living in northern Michigan." Each consists of a simple
proposition about the world combined with a claim about me.

16

For example, to say "I know that the capital of Sc\
Edinburgh" combines a statement of fact (or rathe\
something represented as a fact) about the world - ⌐. ɥɪ
is the capital of Scotland" – with a report on a relationship
between that statement and me – namely, that I know it.
Know in this usage conveys something like a proprietary
interest: I *have* this fact, I *possess* it, I *own* it, though usually
not exclusively. Unfortunately, not every use of *know* is like
that. We also say "I know you." "I know how to make excellent
martinis." "I know that my Redeemer liveth." These are all
more complicated events.

Rather than "I know that it is Tuesday," however, I might say
"I *think* that it is Tuesday," or I might say "I *believe* that it is
Tuesday," each time conveying a different meaning. Moreover,
"I believe that it is Tuesday" has a different feel from "I believe
that Elvis is alive." It is these sorts of differences I wish to
think about.

We also say things like "I consider that [something or other]."
"I feel that...." "I hold that...." "I imagine that...." I don't
propose to examine all these. Some careful consideration of
know and *believe* in their common uses will suffice to make my
point.

I don't want to overcomplicate the question, so let's try a
simple approach. Let's suppose that there is a simple linear
continuum across which propositions may be distributed. Those
that I judge to be certainly true are at one end, those that I
judge to be certainly untrue at the other, and the rest are
scattered in between depending on the degree of credence I
decide to grant them. We might imagine something like this:

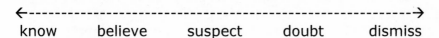

| know | believe | suspect | doubt | dismiss |

We might even imagine that this is not merely a filing system for propositions but part of the judgment apparatus. The line might actually be part of some inner gauge. We take some proposition that has come our way, hook it up to the truth gauge, and the arrow comes to rest at some point along the line, telling us what to think about the proposition, where to file it, and how to use it.

This mechanical sort of model is appealingly simple and might be helpful in some very general, very schematic way, but it surely doesn't really describe what is going on inside the mind. It doesn't feel right. In reflecting on the process of judging, on how judgments emerge or occur in the course of ordinary life, I have no sense of any such procedure. I don't feel myself holding propositions, one by one, up against some such measuring device and reading off a judgment from a meter. On further reflection, moreover, I'm not at all sure that I can arrange my various kinds of judgment along a single dimension like this.

The act of judging the truth of a proposition must certainly involve more than a single criterion, and it would not be surprising if different criteria required different scales and even scales that are in some ways incommensurable. With only an ordinary practitioner's knowledge of the psychology of judgment, we can guess pretty confidently that among the criteria we may bring to bear in a particular instance of judgment are logic (does the proposition make sense in its own terms?), consistency with experience (does it make sense within what we already know of the world?), consistency with the current context (does it make sense in terms of some hypothesis being tested?), personal appeal (is it congenial to our own outlook on the world?), interest (is it to our advantage that it be true?), and so on. We can guess further that there is some calculus that weighs the proposition against some set of criteria like these and arrives at a complex sum that places it at the appropriate point on the scale. And yet it remains true that I am seldom aware of any measuring or calculating going on as I arrive at a judgment. Even that purely conventional phrase seems wrong; more often it seems to me that the judgment arrives at me – it appears in my consciousness, whence I am not sure. It is only afterward, in reflection, that I may trace out some elements of the judgment and infer some of the premises and procedures by which it may have emerged.

Suppose I have been traveling around the world on business, stopping at frequent though irregular intervals to visit local offices and, because of the intricacies of scheduling, sometimes doubling back before continuing on in a generally easterly direction. It's altogether plausible that at some point, on being asked what day it is, I will be uncertain. I will not automatically say "It's Tuesday." I will stop and try to calculate, but from fatigue and confusion about the International Date Line I will hesitate to put my result as a firm answer. I will say "I think it's Tuesday." The word *think* will convey to my interlocutor my uncertainty, and she will thus be put on notice that my answer is to be taken as tentative, provisional. If I have made this trip many times before, however, and have developed both physical endurance and a knack for chronometry, I may be pretty confident in my answer. I may then say "I believe it's Tuesday," meaning to impart a higher level of confidence to the other. A very simple case like this looks as though it could be fitted to the simple linear scale of credence we just imagined.

What about "I believe that Elvis is alive"? Can we point to a spot on that same scale where that statement belongs? Let's begin with "I know that Elvis is alive." Assuming always the full sincerity of the speaker and thus the complete absence of either intent to deceive or irony, this proposition seems to belong in the same part of the scale as "I know that it's Tuesday." But where the shift from "I know that it's Tuesday" to "I believe that it's Tuesday" seems to be simply one of decreasing certainty, moving rightward along that single dimension of credence represented by our line diagram, the shift from "I know that Elvis is alive" to "I believe that Elvis is alive" seems different. The word *believe* in a context like this seems to be carrying some additional significance, some meaning that requires a different scale. There is some force behind it, a force perhaps expressed vocally by emphasis. More or less explicitly, the speaker is reaching beyond knowledge to assert something to be true even in the absence of the usual sorts of evidence. In other words, she is expressing faith.

> Seeing is believing – or so they say. In fact, the proposition is nonsensical. Seeing is knowing, whereas believing is trusting to the existence of something we cannot see. But belief can be stronger than knowing. When we trust to the unseen, we confer power. Deities and subatomic particles and, more recently, the silicon pathways webbed into microchips – all of these we invest with a potency that we do not always grant to more objectively verifiable phenomena.
> – Sven Birkerts

As if these ambiguities were not enough, there is yet an entirely other class of complications. We have proceeded so far as though language were a kind of proposition-generating machine and the propositions thus generated were simply attempts to state what is the case, modified in some instances by an expression of the proposer's degree of confidence in the accuracy of the statement. We know, however, that language is no such value-free machine and that many sentences convey meanings and intentions other than mere reportage, external or internal.

Take, for example, the sentence "Remember the *Maine*!" Does it require or ask for assent? Can I decide that I agree with it and thenceforth declare "I know that remember the *Maine*"? No; that is clearly nonsense. Or take this one: "These are the times that try men's souls." I might say that I agree with the speaker, but I would hesitate to say that I know that these are just that sort of troublous times and not some other kind. Why the hesitation? What sort of agreement would I be offering if I abstain at the same time from granting that such-and-such is the case? Part of the answer is that what I carelessly call my agreement is rather more like sympathy with the sentiment that I detect behind the sentence. Another part of the answer is that the sentence doesn't present a fact; it offers no claim about what is the case that I could either affirm or deny. It is, in other words, not a proposition. It is rhetoric.

Setting aside the many shades of meaning of "know" and "believe" and leaving aside, too, the various social circumstances that lead us to create and then to choose among those shades, let's assume that there is a single, simple, core meaning for each word. What is that meaning? And what determines which one I use in a given case? In other words, when – under what conditions – do I say "I know that *x*," and when – under what other conditions – do I say "I believe that *x*"?

This ought to be easy. I say "I know that *x*" when, well, I *know* it. I *know* that two and two are four. I *know* that Edinburgh is the capital of Scotland. And so on and on. These are true statements. They state something that is the case, meaning that what they propose corresponds to the actual state of affairs. And I know them – that is, I possess them in some way, hold them in my mind. In short: I have a true statement in mind, and so I can say that I know something about the world. Easy.

But no. I am left with a big problem, and it isn't the one the philosophers in the crowd are jumping up and down about. They want to say – scream – that is all too, too simple-minded and begs any number of enormous questions. They are right, of course. How, for example, did I get to the point of having a proposition that could claim to say something about the world? And how was the judgment made that it is a true proposition? How do I know "what is the case" apart from the proposition that states it? What does it mean to say that some verbal formula (such as these black marks on paper: "Edinburgh is the capital of Scotland") corresponds to some state of affairs in the world (such as that certain persons or institutions reside in the physical city called Edinburgh)? These are tough questions that for now I'm quite happy to sidestep. (I'll continue to sidestep them in that I certainly won't solve them and in that they do not affect our practical concerns much. I will return to them later, though, for they are an important part of the backdrop against which the practical business of knowing plays out.)

The problem I want to think about is this: What if I am wrong? What if, in the terms we've adopted here, I have some proposition x in mind and x is not the case – what it asserts does not correspond to the actual state of affairs in the real world – but I treat it as though it is and does? Suppose the proposition is "Moscow is the capital of the Soviet Union" and that I possess this proposition, hold it in mind, accept it as a true statement. I will then say, if prompted, "I know that Moscow is the capital of the Soviet Union." Is there any sign, any warning label for consumers of propositions, that marks this one as anything other than true, as one that should be handled with care? Something that offsets my "I know that..."? No, of course not. It is an unfortunate but inescapable fact that propositions, most of them, just sit there, and unless we have some particular reason not to, we accept them, take them in and give them a home. When we do – and here is my point –

we treat them all alike. This may be a good policy toward pets or children, but it does poorly with propositions.

> Think of what you're saying.
> You can get it wrong and still you think that
> it's all right.
> —Lennon and McCartney

There is another way to treat propositions, one that in fact we use fairly frequently, and that is not to adopt them outright but to take them in, as it were, on probation. We treat them as possible adoptees. Interestingly, we sometimes say that we "entertain" such propositions, recognizing their tentative and guest status. We can then go on to apply various tests of pedigree and employment prospects and so on, perhaps eventually to accept it fully into the family.

But I am setting that approach aside, too, for now in order to concentrate on the special but by no means unusual case in which I have (with or without a prior probationary period) accepted a proposition, taken it in, made it mine. I know that x; but, outside my knowledge, x is false.

> To *know* is one thing, and to know for
> certain *that* we know is another.
> —William James

We become aware of such cases in retrospect. Something occurs to show us that x is false; x, which we held so dear. We were wrong. I've been trying to think of a personal example by way of illustration, but evidently I shall have to make something up. Suppose that up until last Tuesday I held to the proposition that Elvis was born in Memphis, Tennessee. Somehow, sometime, I had encountered that proposition and had embraced it, taken it in as a true statement about the world. (Actually, I may never have encountered that proposition. I may have confused two different propositions or in some other way misremembered.) I may or may not have subjected it to a probationary period, but if I did it had long since passed and the proposition had become a member of the family. On Tuesday, though, perhaps while watching a PBS special, I encountered a conflicting proposition: Elvis was born in Tupelo, Mississippi. Because I am a reasonable person, the PBS endorsement pretty much forces me to accept this new proposition as true, as fact. (I may, again because I am a reasonable person but also perhaps because I don't really give up that easily, double-check in my nearby encyclopedia.) OK, so Elvis was from Tupelo, not Memphis. Live and learn. But what now of the proposition "Elvis was born in Memphis"? And, more interestingly, what has been my relationship to it? That is, what of "I know that Elvis was born in Memphis"?

It's easy enough for me to say now "I know that Elvis was not born in Memphis." But that's not the same proposition; it is what logicians call the contrary. Watch what happens when I try to state my present relationship to the original proposition: I say "I no longer believe that Elvis was born in Memphis." I could say "I no longer know that...." but I don't. In distancing myself from it I also change verbs. Because it is not a true statement I cannot now know it, and I seem to be acknowledging – now – that I never did know it, though I thought that I did. (And what is going on with that word "thought"? Where did it come from? I didn't just *think* that I knew it back then; I *knew* that I knew it.) This is a tough family – you're OK while you're in, but once you're out we don't even know you.

If I reflect on my state of mind before Tuesday, and if I am honest, I have to admit that I knew it. That is, I accepted it completely and without question. If I place the proposition "Elvis was born in Memphis" alongside one that says "I was born in St. Louis," I must acknowledge that they had fully equal standing, that they were truly siblings. Two true statements about the world. That was then.

And now? One of them I still know in exactly the same way, and it feels exactly the same to me as it did before. The other I now want to disavow and to own up, tacitly, that I didn't really know it then, I only believed it. But it didn't seem so then. Was there no way to distinguish between the two, between the knowing and the believing, back then? It might be suggested that the Elvis proposition came to me from outside sources and that I might prudently have held it off at arm's length, as at least possibly unreliable, and thus kept the proposition under probation longer. (How long? Or would it have to have been permanent?) But I have to admit that the other proposition came to me also by way of report – parents and other relatives consistently said it was so, and I have still a piece of official-looking paper that says so. And I have to concede that, at least in principle, they could all have been mistaken or been conspiring to mislead me. Having so admitted and conceded, however, I still know that I was born in St. Louis. (Well, I believe I know I was, anyway.)

> The Old-Fellow was one day in Dingle buying tobacco and tasting spirits, when he heard news which amazed him. He did not believe it because he never trusted the people of that town. The next day he was selling herrings in the Rosses and had the same news from them there; he then half-accepted the story but did not altogether swallow it. The third day he was in Galway city and the story was there likewise. At last he believed it believingly....
> —Flann O'Brien

I make the concession of saying that I believe it, I think, because I am temporarily abashed by the Elvis thing. I was wrong. I have harbored error, like a traitor or at least a wayward relative, in my inner home. For the moment, anyway, I'm aware of my own fallibility and eager to avoid a repetition. This feeling will pass, and tomorrow, if you ask me if I know where I was born, I will say "Yes, of course I do!" Would any number of Elvis-like experiences teach me to say instead "Well, I'm pretty sure I do"?

The philosopher Ludwig Wittgenstein made the characteristically curious observation that "If there were a verb meaning 'to believe falsely,' it would not have any significant first person present indicative." What he meant was simply that it is not possible for me to be in the position of saying "I believe x" while knowing at the same time that x is not true. (Occasions when I may intend to deceive are a different matter.) But what happens, apparently, is that when I am in a position to say "I believe x," thereby implying that I know x to be true, then I want to jump directly to saying "I know x," forgetting that the first instance of knowing, the one that permits the belief, may be mistaken. Maybe it's the going public that is the problem.

It has sometimes occurred, usually in some such informal setting as a party, that someone, on hearing my job title or just the general nature of my work, says "Well, you must know everything!" To which there is no rational response; one can only look smug or try for a becoming modesty, depending on one's mood or chemical state at the time. But sometimes a demonstration will be required that I "know" things. The someone may be inspired to test me by saying, for example, "So, you'd know about the War of Jenkins' Ear, right?" And if I accept the challenge and say, with studied casualness, "Oh, yes – 1642, wasn't it?" my opponent (for that he is, this being a kind of game, one in which I stand to win or lose some temporary social standing) will react with surprise and a little disappointment (for he has lost) and maybe a touch of respect. Why? Because he's done this before. He's played this game in one form or another many times because he knows that almost no one has heard of the War of Jenkins' Ear, hence he will usually win. (One challenge for him, obviously, is to find a way to initiate the game. I was a sitting duck. Another challenge is to keep getting himself invited to parties, despite this behavior.)

But what has actually happened in this exchange that has to do with *knowing*? A phrase is uttered – "the War of Jenkins' Ear." Another phase is offered in return – "sixteen forty-two." Both players agree that the response is appropriate. At this level it does not much differ from many other social rituals like cheering at a football game or singing along with television commercials.

Apart from knowing a correct verbal response to this especially obscure call, what else is it supposed that I know? Suppose that this game actually leads to a conversation about the War of Jenkins' Ear. My opponent (though possibly he is now my teammate, if others are still listening) might say "West Indies, right?" And I might nod (knowingly, of course) and respond "Spanish and English colonists, I think" (I am being charmingly modest.) One of us might go on to mention who this unfortunate Jenkins was. (Or not; we will surely have lost our audience by now.)

We all recognize this category of information as, in a social setting, anyway, trivia, and there are more formal games that employ it. One may even win large sums of money this way (not to mention meeting Regis Philbin), though I have not. Some people are quite adept at trivia. The requirements for success are fairly simple: a retentive memory and a large amount of factual data input over the years. One then is in position to enliven almost any situation by noting that

President Grover Cleveland's actual first name was Stephen, or that the peanut is neither a pea nor a nut.

But again, apart from the mental associations that permit me to link "1642" with "War of Jenkins' Ear," what do I know? Even as I add phrases like "South Carolina" and "Spanish colonists," drawing on further associations stored up years ago, what do I show of knowledge? Do I really *know* something here? And, taking a different tack, what would count as knowledge of the War of Jenkins' Ear? Being able to recite the casualty count? Naming the participants? Explaining the causes and results, as I may have read about them in some history book? At what point could I claim to actually *know* something? (Fairness obliges me to concede, on the other hand, that this sort of thing can be a part of knowing. A colleague of mine who is far better at it than I am and who is widely and truly knowledgeable about many things holds that it is a matter of knowing not just the generalities but "the details.")

Suppose that the War of Jenkins' Ear actually took place in 1645 and that I misremembered the date. In the trivia game, my opponent may have the correct date in mind and may be confident enough to challenge me; or he may also have an incorrect date in mind, though a different one, and be confident enough nonetheless to challenge; or he may have either the correct or an incorrect date in mind but lack the confidence to challenge; or he may have the same incorrect date in mind as I, and unjustifiably concede the point. Clearly, the game does not depend on information alone, or even on correct information alone. If challenged, I may or may not concede, depending on my degree of subjective certainty – my confidence in my own memory. Eventually we may appeal to authority; perhaps there is a set of *Britannica* nearby?

Now suppose that I confess to you that in inventing this imagined social encounter I knew all along that the War of Jenkins' Ear took place neither in 1642 nor in 1645 but really in 1739. I lied. If you stopped reading before this paragraph, if perhaps you put down the book to get ready for a party, and if at that party you fell into conversation with someone who brought up the War of Jenkins' Ear (it could happen!), and if you decided to enter the game and said "Ah, yes, 1642, wasn't it?" then maybe you lost the game, for which I apologize. But maybe you didn't lose. Either way, you didn't know what you thought you knew. You believed it, but you didn't know it.

But you know it now, right? Or do you? Maybe you should look it up before the next party.

> It isn't what a man knows, but what he thinks he knows that he brags about. Big talk means little knowledge.
> –George Horace Lorimer

Let's take another look at "I *know that* something or other." First, there is the factual proposition, the something-or-other part, such as "Edinburgh is the capital of Scotland." Given that we agree on the meaning of this sentence (easily given for many conventional matters, such as the Edinburgh case, but not always so), it is either true or false. Then, there is the assertion "*I know that....*" This one lives on two levels. There is first the level on which I report truly or not on the state of my knowledge: I am sincere in claiming to know, or I am not. Then there is the matter of whether the proposition matches the actual case. Letting x stand for the candidate factual statement, the various possibilities may be listed this way:

1. I know that
   x.   [I am sincere]
   [and x is true]

2. I know that
   x.   [I am sincere]
   [but x is false]

3. I know that   [I'm kidding you]
           x.   [and x is false]

4. I know that   [I'm kidding you]
           x.   [but x is true anyway]

Of the four cases, I state a falsehood in two (2 and 3) and in a third (4) I state the truth accidentally and unawares. In two cases (2 and 4) I think I know what I don't know. In three out of four either I am mistaken or I mislead, or both. Not good odds if you are trying to decide whether to believe me or not based just on probabilities. This analysis is reasonably straightforward when x is, in fact, true; but watch what happens when it is false. Let's let x = "Elvis was born in Memphis." Now the two cases where x is true drop out, leaving cases 2 and 3, the ones in which, intentionally or not, I mislead you. But our concern here is not with deception but with knowing, whatever that may be. Case 3 is one in which, whatever I may think to be so, my intention is to persuade you that I know x, which implies that x is true, when in fact I know that it is not, or, in the notation of symbolic logic, I know $\sim x$. This leaves case 2, in which I sincerely...what? Know? Surely we don't want to say that I know something that is not the case. So I sincerely believe, not just x, but that *I know* x. My belief is so sincere that I no longer think of it as belief but simply as knowing.

But I'm wrong. I am in error. And it is of the essence of being in error that I don't know it. Not only do I not know that I am in error, I positively believe that I am not. I believe that I am correct, that I am possessed of the truth. No, that's not strong enough. I don't merely believe that I am correct, I know it! For me, belief doesn't enter into the matter. I damned well *know*.

But I'm still wrong.

3: common senses

> For now we see through a glass, darkly.
> —St. Paul

Let's assume that it is possible to know something. (In the next chapter, having thrown in the towel on any hope of proving something, I'll try to construct a very elaborate rationalization for making such as assumption.) If it is possible to know, so that we can talk about knowledge as something real, where would such knowledge as we are able to acquire be coming from? That is, given that I know *x* (remember: we're assuming I can); how did *x* get into my head? The possible sources might be sorted into three categories: (1) *x* was already, and therefore always, in my head; (2) *x* came from the world outside me; or (3) *x* came from outside the world.

Category (3) is obviously the most problematic. What is "outside the world"? It is not obvious that the phrase actually means anything, but if it does, what does it indicate and, more to our point, what could come from there? Well, revelation for one thing. Various individuals throughout history have asserted that they possessed knowledge that had been imparted to them directly from some unworldly source, such as God or a god, or that they had acquired by such means as meditation or divination. Knowledge from such sources is, on the evidence, very compelling to those who receive and accept it; it is less so, in varying degrees, to the rest of us. I'm going to set it aside for now.

Category (1) constitutes an issue that occupied philosophers and, eventually, psychologists for centuries. It is usually referred to as the doctrine of innate ideas. The question may be posed this way: Does the mind come into the world with any content at all, or is it purely a receptacle (or, not so purely, a receptacle adapted to receive certain kinds of content, and perhaps also connected to some sort of processor) for what it will receive from outside itself? You may have wondered this yourself, as I have, and if you are like me, you have probably shrugged and said, in effect, "I don't know, and I don't think it likely that I ever will." It's just this sort of nonchalant attitude that disqualifies us from being philosophers. The professionals have gone at this question like terriers – lots of energy, lots of noise, lots of holes all over the yard, but no bone.

Plato, for example, was very clear that there are innate ideas, as was Descartes. Locke said no; he referred to the mind as a *tabula rasa*, a blank slate, on which the world of experience writes its lessons. Others analyzed, distinguished, hedged, all the things that philosophers do when they are at work. One of the interesting hedges, accomplished by Immanuel Kant among others, was to say that there might not be innate ideas, in the sense of actual concepts or practical knowledge, but that there are certain categories, or modes of thinking, that are built in. For Kant, space and time were such categories; as he saw it, everything that we experience and every thought that we subsequently have about that experience, is structured in terms of space and time, and we cannot have either experience or thought outside those categories. What makes this interesting from a contemporary point of view is that it can be fitted without too much bending or folding to modern neuroscience, which increasingly finds itself understanding mental phenomena in terms of the inbuilt characteristics, the wiring, of particular structures or regions in the brain.

Fortunately for us amateur brain-users, we don't have to solve this problem. Unless we take the position that all knowledge is innate, which puts us in the black hole of the solipsists, whence nothing logically issues (more of them later), then we're left with the case in which some or all of what we know comes from the world. For a variety of reasons (some of which we will examine) this seems to me the most reasonable view, and it is the case I will address in this chapter.

If it is true, then, that some or most or all of what we know originates outside us, in the world, how does it get in? The conventional answer is, by means of the senses. A "sense," according to my dictionary, is "a faculty of perceiving" or "a specialized ... function or mechanism (as sight, hearing, smell, taste, or touch) basically involving a stimulus and a sense organ." There is a bit of tautology in these definitions, as there often is in dictionary definitions. That is, they seem to circle around and reformulate the term of interest without telling us anything new. Let me propose a definition of my own: "a physical channel by which information in some specific medium is conveyed to the brain (or mind, if you prefer)."

The examples given in the dictionary definition – sight, hearing, smell, taste, or touch – are the conventional "five senses." The identification of precisely five human senses goes back at least to Aristotle, who discussed each of them at length (and in precisely the order preserved in the dictionary) in his *Peri psyches* ("On the Soul"). Because of the enormous weight that Aristotelian science carried in Western culture at least until the emergence of modern experimental science, the notion of there being five and only five senses persisted and was incorporated into the body of everyday speech. (Book III of "On the Soul" begins thus: "That there is no sixth sense in addition to the five enumerated – sight, hearing, smell, taste, touch – may be established by the following considerations:" followed by some elaborate argumentation. Aristotle also considers that "It might be asked why we have more senses than one.") Because of the commonplace understanding that there are but five senses, the phrase "sixth sense" came to be used to suggest some mysterious, nonphysical mode of apprehension, a supernatural (or "extrasensory") access to knowledge that falls into our third category above.

33

But are there just five? Take sight, for example. Aristotle devoted most of his discussion of sight to explaining the sensation of color, which is certainly peculiar to and characteristic of sight. But what of motion? Detecting the motion of objects seems quite different from and unrelated to the perception of color, though both occur through the medium of light and by means of the mechanisms of the eye. And neurobiology confirms that quite distinct parts of the visual system are involved. Might "sight" actually be a convenient term for a group of distinguishable senses?

Hearing seems to be pretty much a single sense. High pitches or low, loud or soft, pure or complex, all seem to be the discriminations of a single faculty, even though the task is accomplished by different kinds of mechanism in different species. In the human ear, however, there is additional machinery, the nonauditory labyrinth or vestibular organ, that detects acceleration, rotation, and orientation in a gravitational field. This "vestibular sense" is the one that tells you that you are upright or not, at rest or falling, and it's the one that makes the rollercoaster fun (or not, as the case may be). Lacking a rollercoaster with which to experience the alternative, Aristotle didn't imagine a sense dedicated to telling him he was standing still.

He also didn't notice, or didn't deem worth discussing, the fact that he always knew where his arms and legs were, even with his eyes closed and even if some outside force moved them without his conscious effort. Surely this awareness of where your various parts are is a sense, too? Indeed, psychologists refer to this and some related sorts of bodily awareness as "kinesthetic sense."

Touch is perhaps the easiest sense to decompose into more specific senses, which collectively are sometimes referred to as the "cutaneous senses," meaning simply that they are lodged in the skin. In a restrictive sense, "touch" refers to one of these, the ability to detect pressure on the skin (which, on the basis of experiment, further turns out to be at least two different senses in that very light pressure and deep stimulation are detected by different means). Receptors in the skin can also detect heat and cold (separately, to some extent); mechanical deformation; and pain.

So how many senses are there? The answer depends on how we define "sense," whether more exactingly than the dictionary or not. In the end, however, it makes little difference how we count them. Like all categories, the one labeled "the senses" is only as good as it is useful. What is of importance for our present purpose is to understand what it is that the senses do, and what they don't do.

I offered my own definition of "sense" a few paragraphs back: "a physical channel by which information in some specific medium is conveyed to the brain (or mind, if you prefer)." Thinking of the senses as instances of information system permits us to borrow some handy ideas and terminology without worrying much about anatomy and what is not yet understood about the physiology of perception. The basic concept in information theory might be depicted as follows:

source--→encoder----[message]--→decoder--→receiver

In words, something – a body, a system – emits energy in some form in the course of undergoing some process. The emitted energy is of a nature and is modulated in a way that are characteristic of the particular process. (The modulation may or may not be purposeful, that is, it may or may not be done with intent to send a message.) Later, the energy is absorbed by some other something that is not only able to interact physically with that kind of energy but is able to respond to the way it is modulated in order to extract meaning from it. A simple example: In a particular star a process of nuclear fusion releases electromagnetic energy with a characteristic range of wavelengths; the energy propagates through space for a while, and eventually some of it strikes a particular object that absorbs some of it and reflects some of it; the portion that is reflected, and the manner in which it is reflected, are characteristic of the particular object and of some other circumstances; a portion of what is reflected then passes into your eye, strikes your retina, excites certain nerve cells that are sensitive to electromagnetic waves of those wavelengths, causing electrical impulses to travel along nerve paths to a module in the brain that transforms the particular pattern of impulses it receives into an impression of a certain kind. In short, the Sun shines and you see, let us say, a fig newton.

The senses are the means by which we take part in this transaction. They are our points of contact with the outer world, the paths by which information originating outside us reaches the decoding machine inside us. That machine, we believe, is the brain, and although we don't know much about how it works we do know some things, such as that the senses all seem to convert the particular sort of energy to which they are responsive – electromagnetic, acoustic, thermal – into nerve impulses, which travel by a combination of electrical and chemical processes to the brain. And we know that in the brain there seems to be a variety of distinguishable regions where signals from the senses and other internal sources are processed – decoded – in special ways to produce particular effects. In the case of signals originating in the senses, the effects are what we call perceptions, of light, of sound, of warmth, and so on.

Our very incomplete understanding of this phenomenon of sense perception is matter for other books. I wish here to make four points about it: (1) it works; (2) we believe in it; (3) although we can't figure out how to justify ourselves in words, we *should* believe in it; and (4) what it tells us is nonetheless partial and uncertain. As to that fourth point: Trust me; a little paradox is good for you.

It works. Well, doesn't it? You see the cookie. That is, you experience a visual perception consisting of a large variety of varicolored patches that seem placed *out there* in various directions and at sundry distances; attending to one limited set of those colored patches, you interpret it (without consciously considering the matter) as constituting an integrated system of the general kind known as "physical object" and of the specific sort called "cookie," and somehow by merely willing it to occur you extend a hand in a direction and to a distance calculated (without consciously calculating) to correspond to those of the "cookie," and by further willing you close your fingers, which send back yet more perceptions of a tactile kind that you interpret as the physical presence of the object in your grasp. You then conduct the "cookie" through space to a point just below that from which you seem to be seeing this drama, will some more complicated motions, and are rewarded with still another perception which causes you pleasure of the gustatory kind that you would, if asked, explain as "It tastes good."

Person eats cookie. An utterly ordinary event, made possible by a set of energetic interactions that become more and more complex and mysterious the closer they are examined. And yet, however mysterious it may seem, however difficult it may be to comprehend, it is equally hard to imagine how it could be otherwise. Consider: In a world in which organic evolution is possible, and in which consequently the organisms that evolve compete for energy, there is an obvious advantage in being able to detect and thus obtain desirable energy sources more efficiently than do others. Where physical distance is one common obstacle to be overcome, the advantage naturally falls to those organisms possessed of some means of detection over distance, making use of such energy flows as may happen to exist in that world: reflected electromagnetic radiation, acoustic signals, or the like. Any organism that happened to develop some rudimentary means of detection, some simple sensing organ, would be favored to survive and reproduce its kind over those that were obliged to rely on fortuitously bumping into things. Not guaranteed, mind; just favored. There is evidence that in the course of biological evolution on Earth, visual organs have evolved not once but many times, in many different lines, and this is not surprising in view of the very great utility of vision in finding food and avoiding becoming food.

When contemplating evolution we are apt to think in terms of gooey swamp water filled with unnameable little swimming things, or alternatively in terms of doomed dinosaurs browsing on cycads or each other. We are less apt to think of our own human senses and faculties. We are apt, that is, to forget that

> Like all other forms of life, humankind
> remains inextricably entangled in flows of
> matter and energy that result from eating
> and being eaten. However clever we have
> been in finding new niches in that system,
> the...balances limiting human access to food
> and energy have not been abolished, and
> never will be.
> —William H. McNeill

to forget, that is, that we are the product of the same process that produced algae, trilobites, and dinosaurs, and therefore are subject to the same imperatives and constraints. Within a process of evolution, powered by continuous variation and refereed by the natural selection that will occur among competing species of differing fitness for a given set of environmental challenges, it would perhaps be more surprising if abilities like vision and hearing did not develop. They may not be bound to (or they may; evolutionists are divided on the point); but if they do, they will tend pretty strongly to be conserved. In short, any species that has gotten as far as humans have (I betray a prejudice here, of course, in thinking of our present condition as fairly advanced) must be pretty well suited to its circumstances, pretty well adapted, that is, to life on Earth. So saying (of the perceptual process) that it works is almost a tautology; if it didn't, we would not likely be here to complain about it.

We believe in it. The foregoing may seem to some readers to stray close to begging the question, the rhetorical maneuver by which one implicitly assumes the conclusion to be proved, disguising the fact as well as one may. I don't actually think that it is, but then I also suspect that begging the question may have an unduly bad reputation. It is clear, though, that no one accepts the evidence of the senses and behaves in accord with it on the basis or as the result of conscious logical (or even illogical) considerations. We see the hand of another reaching for our cookie and we respond – snatch! – without thought or delay. Why?

One simple and attractive possibility is that we are all, at bottom, empiricists. That is, we have observed over many, many instances that acting on the basis of our perceptions is usually rewarded by success: We get the cookie, hence the pleasure. Another word for this process is learning. From infancy, in this theory, we learn by our successes to trust the reports of our senses. This is doubtless correct to some extent. Certainly we learn *how* to act with respect to sensory reports – how to guide the hand to the point where we see the cookie, how to keep hold of it until it reaches our mouth – and in such matters practice makes for as close to perfection as can be. But it may not be the whole story. At the risk of seeming to beg some more questions, I suggest that we may in some further part believe in what our senses report because it makes such a strong, even ineluctable, claim upon us. Most of the time, the field of impressions that our senses bring us is very, very present. It is vivid, commanding, unavoidable. In short, it is *real*. And, note, that when this is so the senses themselves – the faculties of sight, hearing, touch, and so on – are transparent to us, as are indeed the impressions themselves. What we *see* is not vision or visual sense data but things, in the world. What we *hear* is not hearing or acoustical data but sounds. What we *feel* is not touch or tactile sensations but real things on the outside, pressing in upon us. We are wholly unaware of the sensations and the process of perception itself. Only phenomenologists, among the philosophers, and Impressionists, among the artists, attempt to study the sense data themselves.

And again, we can see a *post facto* rationale for our propensity to react directly to the world without first having to calculate probabilities or to remind ourselves that it is, indeed, reality. Natural selection would not treat kindly a species that was as slow as that to respond to the threats or opportunities presented by a fast-moving world.

Note further a crucial fact: The senses work together to weave the world that we perceive. We hear the sound of a baby crying; we turn toward the source of the sound and see a baby; we reach out and find ourselves touching, holding a baby-shaped object just where we see a baby-looking thing from which proceeds the babyish noise. It is not apparent why the various nerve impulses generated by different kinds of receptor cells in different parts of the body and processed in different parts of the brain should somehow agree like this, but they do, most of the time. (If this worries you, and you investigate, you will discover that this is called the "binding problem" by the you-know-whos.) The upshot is that the perceptions given us by the senses are not merely credible but convincing, and utterly so. Apart from those rare and often not especially productive moments when we reflect upon these matters, we live by the grace of the senses immersed in a rich stew of immediate sensation that seems to comprise a world. (It is only fair to note that this "world," whatever it is, seems to have little competition for our attention, again excepting the cases of those few individuals who claim direct contact with another reality.)

We should believe in it. Or have you got a better idea? Alternatives have been proposed, mostly variations on one of two themes, that this world is an inferior sort of reality and that we ought to focus our attention on a higher one, or that the world is altogether illusory and we ought to ditto. Evidence that any of these alternatives constitutes a better idea is slim. To begin with, reports of what the other, superior or true, reality is like tend not to agree very well with one another. They tend also to be short on detail. Most crucially, they tend to consist of mere verbal reports, which lack the compelling vividness, the texture, the presence of the experienced world about us. This is not to say that such views have lacked for audiences and adherents; on the contrary. (We'll look into this again in the next chapter.) But there are degrees of adherence, ranging from the nodding acquiescence that many of us may allow to the full-throttle commitment that very few can manage, and numbers tell us something. Under certain circumstances, one of these views may from time to time elicit a good deal of nodding, but the number of people who proceed actually to behave as if it were true – as if the world were mere illusion or an inferior sort of thing not worthy of attention – is always very, very small.

It has sometimes been argued that when we are dreaming we also seem to be in a real situation, in a real world, although one quite different in texture and logic from the waking world, and that therefore we have no basis on which to declare the waking world to be the really real one. Some entertaining science-fiction stories have taken this point as a premise. Can we really not choose between them? It is not really a practical question at all, of course. A few Romantic poets aside, hardly anyone has ever sought to exchange the waking world for a dream world for more than a night at a time. As to distinguishing them in principle, it seems to me a crucial point that when I am in the waking world I am aware of the existence (in some sense) of both, and have an explanation for both, but when I am in the dream world it alone seems to exist. This points to a certain poverty in the dream world. Moreover, from my waking stance I can compare the quality of the experience of the two and decide that the waking world is more developed, more complex, more convincing overall than the other one. I also like the continuity of the waking world, whereby the one I awake to each morning is so very much like the one I left last night. It is usually convenient to be able to pick up where one left off. The dream world is too fractured and unpredictable for my taste, and often as not I find I can't remember it.

So, on the evidence, it seems prudent to act on the basis of sense experience. It works, most of the time (and we even learn, in the course of life, how to recognize a good many of the situations in which it does not) and no demonstrably superior alternative has been proposed. The world exists; it looks pretty much as it seems to; and we are pretty well suited to make our way in it. It's just common sense.

So why does this answer seem glib, all too suspiciously easy?

I alluded to one reason a few paragraphs back: Being the talkative species that we are, we are accustomed to being able to explain things to our own satisfaction and others'. Why is the sky blue? It took some time, but we have a satisfactory answer for that one. Why does the moon loom larger on the horizon? That's still a bit of a puzzle, but we are sure that we will know a good answer when we see it and that we will, sooner or later, see it. Ask a question about any aspect of the world, and we have answered it or we are working on it or we have put it on the list to be worked on. The answers aren't always final, of course. We are also always developing new methods for getting better answers. The point is, we have the habit of success, of being able to come up with answers that seem plausible and useful and more or less right. But questions about the nature of existence as a whole are apparently in a different category, and our tools don't work very well. Descartes was a rigorous thinker, and we can never know whether he was at all embarrassed by having to fall back on assuming the existence of a benevolent God in order to prove the existence of the world (we'll look at this more closely in the next chapter). Most of us cannot accept such an argument as a proof, but we have nothing to offer in its place. Philosophy, reason, language itself – they're just not up to it. But then, there's no particular reason to expect that they would be. They are hammers trying to do the work of a crochet needle.

This is only a problem when we make it one, however. We're a little like someone who has just learned to ride a bicycle: We do fairly well until we start to think about what we're doing, and then we fall. Making it a problem and then trying to solve it is the work of philosophers, who early on saw why it was a hard problem and came up with a name for the tool they would need – metaphysics, meaning something like "talking about nature from outside or above" – even though they haven't yet built the tool itself.

Another reason it seems too easy to say that we can simply sit back and trust to the evidence of our senses, of course, is that sometimes we can't. This brings us to a really big On the Other Hand, namely...

Perception is partial and uncertain. A problem, a real problem, that we all experience from time to time stems directly from the "realness" of the perceived world, that utterly convincing quality it has, composed in part of the vividness of our impressions and in part of the apparently seamless way they fit together to form a whole rather than a collection of separate sensations.

(I wonder if it would even be possible for the world to seem any other way? Could there be a perceived world with, so to speak, holes in it? If the world consists wholly of those perceptions brought in through the senses, how would the spaces between perceptions be perceived, unless there were a sense able to do just that? And why would there be such a sense? After all, on a dark night our world doesn't become a different one from the daylight world, composed now only of train whistles and dog barking and traffic noises with great voids in between. It's the same world, only dark. We fill in where we can't see.)

Anyway, this problem: Despite the fact that It Works, the truth is that once in a while It Doesn't. Once in a while we see something that isn't there, meaning that nothing shows up on our other senses, especially not the bumping-into detector. Once in a while we don't see something that is there, meaning that we may well bump into it, to our surprise and perhaps injury. We hear things, we feel things, we smell things that we later judge to have been figments, illusions, imaginings. Why? And more to the point, what does this say about our premise?

There are many ways in which the senses can be fooled, some fairly well understood and some not at all. Some have to do with the actual structural details of the sensing organs. A number of common optical illusions (you've seen the ones with parallel lines that seem to converge or equal-length lines that seem different) exploit the way lines are detected and coded in the retina of the eye. Some apparently work at a higher level where pattern detection goes on, such as the drawing of a vase that suddenly becomes two faces in profile. Some derive from purely external causes, such as the physics of light waves that produces the illusion of a wet patch on the road ahead of us on a hot day. (A more subtle effect stems from the fact that some sense organs are sensitive to more than one kind of stimulus but can only respond in one way. There are cells in the mouth that seem intended to function as detectors of high, potentially damaging, temperature, but they turn out to be highly sensitive also to the compound capsaicin, found in the members of the pepper family so popular in tropical cuisines. The presence of capsaicin in food is signaled as a sensation of "hot" that has nothing to do with temperature.)

Doubtless it was the awareness of such phenomena, which afflict everyone but with which everyone learns to cope, that helped provoke philosophical speculation as to the reality of the external world in the first place. Descartes certainly mentions the occurrence of illusions among the reasons to begin systematically doubting everything. Does the existence of error of this kind really call everything into question? Does the fact that we make mistakes in arithmetic threaten the foundations of mathematics? Only if you're looking for trouble.

But if it does not turn us into solipsists, it should give us pause. If what we know of reality is based on what is conveyed to us by the senses, and if the senses are fallible, then the prudent person will begin his list of Rules to Know By with something like "Be aware of the possibility of observational error." Some kinds of observational error are common enough that we become familiar with them early and learn to adjust for them. Experienced drivers don't hit the brakes when they "see" that "wet" patch ahead. (And even this learned behavior is a matter of substituting one rule of thumb for another, and this can equally lead to error. Sometimes that "wet" patch is really a wet patch.) Other kinds of observational error may take even the most experienced observer by surprise.

With this caveat, are we in a position to say then that our senses give us a pretty thorough picture of reality? That the perceived world matches up nicely, pretty much point for point, with what's really out there? Not quite.

robert mchenry

About 800 years ago it was found that a piece of lodestone (an iron-bearing rock that is naturally magnetic) floated on a stick in water would rotate so as to point north and south. The usefulness of such a trick for navigators was quickly apparent, but it was not understood for hundreds of years why it worked. Eventually, scientists developed the notion of magnetism, a force that is intangible and invisible but can seem to act over distance on certain kinds of matter, notably iron and some other metals, and then the idea of the magnetic field, a way of conceptualizing the varying strength and direction of magnetism in a volume of space. During that same period, the practical needs of navigators and other travelers pushed the development of more and more accurate and sophisticated compasses to exploit whatever it was that made them behave so. Although we are all familiar with magnets and magnetism, they still seem, on reflection, mysterious. Think of when, as a child, you tried to push two similarly aligned magnets together and felt them repel each other, although you could see nothing between them but air. Is magnetism, then, something unworldly or extrasensory? It certainly has sometimes been considered so. Only in comparatively recent times has it been suspected, and only very recently has evidence been discovered, that pigeons sense the Earth's magnetic field and use that sense to orient themselves, thus being capable of finding their ways home from great distances and arbitrary directions.

Do pigeons have, then, a theory of magnetism? A concept of the field? Do they suspect the relation of the magnetic field to the electrical one? Probably not. Such intellectual achievements seem to be the exclusive province of humans (on Earth, anyway). The point here is that we had to find these things out indirectly because we are blind (or deaf, or something) ourselves to magnetism. We can't distinguish a bar magnet from an otherwise identical but nonmagnetic piece of metal without performing an experiment and inferring the magnetism from the result. When I take two magnets and try to push their like poles (north-north, south-south) together I can feel the resistance, a mechanical effect of magnetic repulsion, and because I am insensitive to the magnetism itself this resistance seems mysterious. The space between the magnets, which to a pigeon evidently has some sensible characteristic, it to me completely empty, a sensory blank. Unless I can contrive to transform magnetic phenomena into the quite different kinds of phenomena which I am equipped to sense, I remain unaware of magnetism altogether. Somehow, pigeons sense magnetism. We may imagine that they feel it, or smell it, but these are analogies to our senses and surely do not capture what it is like to sense magnetism. We'll never have that experience. Likewise, we cannot sense electrical fields, as some sharks do, or see ultraviolet, as bees do, and moreover we cannot even imagine what it might be like if we could.

In discussing a similar case, Thomas Nagel described our situation in this way:

> Now we know that most bats (the microchiroptera, to be precise) perceive the external world primarily by sonar, or echolocation, detecting the reflections, from objects within range, of their own rapid, subtly modulated, high-frequency shrieks. Their brains are designed to correlate the outgoing impulses with the subsequent echoes, and the information thus acquired enables bats to make precise discriminations of distance, size, shape, motion, and texture comparable to those we make by vision. But bat sonar, though clearly a form of perception, is not similar in its operation to any sense that we possess, and there is no reason to suppose that it is subjectively like anything we can experience or imagine....It

will not help to try to imagine that one has webbing on one's arms, which enables one to fly around at dusk and dawn catching insects in one's mouth; that one has very poor vision, and perceives the surrounding world by a system of reflected high-frequency sound signals; and that one spends the day hanging upside down by one's feet in an attic. Insofar as I can imagine this (which is not very far), it tells me only what it would be like for *me* to behave as a bat behaves. But that is not the question. I want to know what it is like for a *bat* to be a bat.

Let's go back for a moment to our enumeration of the senses. Whether there are five, or eight, or eighteen is, as we saw, in large part a matter of what we choose to let count as a sense. The number is, in any case, immaterial in light of one simple fact: There aren't as many as there might be. Evolution has given us a few important senses, useful to our organic lives, but there was never any reason to expect that it would equip us to know everything that is going on in the universe. What if we could "see" ultraviolet and infrared and radio and X rays and microwaves and so on? And could sense magnetism and gravity waves and cosmic rays and neutrino radiation and the Higgs field and who-knows-what-else that we haven't yet discovered or imagined? What would the world seem like then?

Our circumstance might be likened to that of a pilot flying a small plane using instruments alone. His information about the world outside is limited in amount and kind to that reported by a few instruments that are sensitive to only certain aspects of that world. He has, for example, an altimeter, a horizon indicator, an airspeed indicator, and a compass. The paltry data they afford him are all he has with which to construct a notion of what is out there, beyond his cockpit. This is a rough analogy at best. In the case of a real pilot, of course, he knows full well how impoverished is this set of information compared with what he might have in other circumstances. He knows what he is missing.

Suppose that our pilot also has radar. The screen presents him with a visual representation of that outer world — or rather, of some simple features of it. What is in that representation, and why? The technology and application of radar in aviation has "evolved" (using the term analogically, too) to fulfill certain critical purposes, and so it is sensitively attuned to those features of the world that bear upon those purposes and is largely blind to any that do not. So, using the radar, the pilot can be informed of the presence of other aircraft in the area, of nearby mountains or tall structures or radar beacons, perhaps of impending rough weather. These appear as spots or patches of light on an otherwise featureless screen. The pilot knows, if he stops to think of it, that if he were to use his own visual system to examine the same scene, say, by looking out the window, he would perceive something quite different. Looking ahead, the radar "sees" an aircraft – not even that, really, but simply a radar-signal-reflecting object, which causes the production of a bright spot on the screen, which is then interpreted by the pilot as representing an aircraft. From the radar the pilot gets no other report. If he looks out the window he may see the aircraft (if it is close enough and it is daylight) and note that it is a yellow Piper Cub with unusual markings; he may well also see a blue sky (most probably a sky exhibiting a range of blue hues), some variety of clouds (including perhaps one that for all the world resembles a whale – or is it a camel?), a vee of geese flapping idly southward, a patchwork of fields below, some green and some brown (in a dozen different shades assorted over a hundred different shapes), patches of woods, meandering streams, roadways, towns, and off at the horizon the beginnings of a spectacular sunset. To all these, of no relevance to its purpose, the radar is quite oblivious. It sees what it needs to see, and a few things more that happen to resemble in some salient but accidental way those that are of crucial interest.

The real pilot knows this. But the hypothetical situation that makes up our analogy might well have featured a pilot who had been born and had grown up in a cockpit with no windows and had consequently never had any view of the outside world other than that offered by the radar and the few other instruments. What would he know of blue skies and sunsets? Our lot as sensing beings is just so. Our perceived – that is, our sensed and construed – world is, thankfully, far richer than that shown on a radar screen, but it is a no less partial representation of reality.

Just as I can infer magnetism by trying to push two magnets together or by noting the tendency of a freely turning magnet to align itself always in a certain direction, we humans have devised a great many ingenious ways of finding out things about the world that our senses would never have revealed. So we know about magnetic fields and electrical fields and ultraviolet radiation and gamma radiation and X rays and quarks and photons and on and on. How we come to know this is matter for later. For now it is sufficient if I can evoke a sense that we inhabit a world richer in content than we know and in which we make our way pretty successfully despite our limited access to what is going on around us. We are immersed in energy flows of who-knows-how-many kinds. Some of them we detect and make use of; some are not meant for us, and we ignore them; and some, it would be prudent to assume, we have yet even to suspect.

In 1884 Edwin A. Abbott published a remarkable little book called *Flatland*, in which he attempted to convey to nonmathematical readers the realization that our three-dimensional world is not necessarily the only possibility. He did this by imagining how an inhabitant of a two-dimensional world, Flatland, would deal with the mind-stretching idea of a third dimension. The book was dedicated this way:

> To
> The Inhabitants of Space in General
> And H.C. in Particular
> This work is Dedicated
> By a Humble Native of Flatland
> In the Hope that
> Even as he was Initiated into the Mysteries
> of Three Dimensions
> Having been previously conversant
> With Only Two
> So the Citizens of that Celestial Region
> May aspire yet higher and higher
> To the Secrets of Four Five or even Six Dimensions
> Thereby contributing
> To the Enlargement of the Imagination
> And the possible Development
> Of that most rare and excellent Gift of Modesty
> Among the Superior Races
> Of Solid Humanity.

The "Gift of Modesty" is no less excellent and appropriate for us.

Early in this chapter we asked how knowledge gets into us and we fixed upon the senses as the channel(s). This was too simple. As became clear in the discussion of the senses, what they convey is information: patterns encoded as signals on energy flows. This is not the same thing as knowledge. Knowledge takes those patterns as raw materials only. Something else is required to produce knowledge, to raise that set of varicolored patches to the existential status of cookie. It is not simply the difference between "I see" and "I know," for even "I see" requires some foundation that remains thereafter for the most part out of sight.

4: believe it!

Some things you suspect, some things you
guess at and some things you just know.
        –Bernie Lincicome

For a variety of mostly good reasons, the word "ideology" has
for most people taken on faintly negative connotations. When
we hear of "ideology" we are apt to think of programs like
communism or identity politics or some other grand cause that
enlists disturbingly avid persons with a loose grip on reality
and poor social skills. The dictionary supports this notion of
ideology: "visionary theorizing" is the first sense, followed by
"the manner or the content of thinking characteristic of an
individual, group, or culture" and "the integrated assertions,
theories and aims that constitute a sociopolitical program." But
almost hidden among these definitions is a more encompassing
one that permits us to use the word ideology for "a systematic
body of concepts esp. about human life or culture." I want to
use that noncommittal definition to rescue the word "ideology,"
with a lowercase i, from the visionaries and revolutionaries of
Big-I Ideologies. We'll come back to them at the end, briefly.

By little-i ideology, then, I mean any systematic means,
consciously applied or otherwise, of organizing our mental life.
Before the application of some ideology, some organizing
principles or patterns, the content of the mind amounts to
sensory impressions and any immediate reflexive responses we
may make, and nothing more. In order to make anything of
that content – to derive meaning, suppose understanding,
make predictions, create a world – some kind of order must be
imposed. In order to do that, assumptions must be made,
though we do not usually recognize them as assumptions. If
we call them anything, we call them "common sense."

common sense the hard way

"For a long time I had remarked that it is sometimes requisite in common life to follow opinions which one knows to be most uncertain, exactly as though they were indisputable." That observation helped lead René Descartes to seek out the ground beneath such opinions, however useful and even necessary they might be, and even beneath the assumptions that are so common that they are unnoticed and unquestioned. In our everyday affairs, in our moment-to-moment conduct, for example, we assume that we are embedded in a world that is *out there* and is distinct from, though somehow related to, what is *in here*. But is it? How do we know that it is? And if we do not *know* it, what justifies our assuming it?

Descartes set forth a methodical approach to finding answers:

> [B]ecause...I wished to give myself entirely to the search after Truth, I thought that it was necessary for me to take an apparently opposite course, and to reject as absolutely false everything as to which I could imagine the least ground of doubt, in order to see if afterwards there remained anything in my belief that was entirely certain. Thus, because our senses sometimes deceive us, I wished to suppose that nothing is just as they cause us to imagine it to be; and because there are men who deceive themselves in their reasoning and fall into paralogisms, even concerning the simplest matters of geometry, and judging that I was as subject to error as was any other, I rejected as false all the reasons formerly accepted by me as demonstrations. And since all the same thoughts and conceptions which we have while awake may also come

> to us in sleep, without any of them being at
> that time true, I resolved to assume that
> everything that ever entered into my mind
> was no more true than the illusions of my
> dreams.

This program of radical doubt is about as rigorous as anyone could conceive. Applying it, Descartes made his first and most famous discovery:

> [W]hilst I thus wished to think all things
> false, it was absolutely essential that the "I"
> who thought this should be somewhat, and
> remarking that this truth *"I think, therefore I
> am"* was so certain and so assured that all
> the most extravagant suppositions brought
> forward by the sceptics were incapable of
> shaking it, I came to the conclusion that I
> could receive it without scruple as the first
> principle of the Philosophy for which I was
> seeking.

On that rock of certainty he proceeded to rebuild his world, logical step by logical step, requiring that each step fulfill just one criterion for truth, "that the things which we conceive very clearly and distinctly are all true." (That this is an adequate idea of truth remains an assumption.)

Very quickly Descartes found himself in trouble. He could not proceed directly to prove to himself the existence of anything outside himself. He had first to construct a proof of the existence of God and then, based on the perfection and therefore goodness of God, deduce that God would not deceive him with perceptions of a nonexistent world. It seems roundabout at first blush, but the difficulty Descartes thereby sidestepped is real.

There is, in fact, a philosophical doctrine that acknowledges the difficulty as insurmountable and simply withdraws from the game. This is the doctrine of solipsism, which holds that only the self exists and that it can know only its own modifications. As a doctrine it is so reduced, so barren, as to be logically unassailable; who has standing to argue a solipsist out of his position? (It is curious to think of a solipsist attempting to make the case for his view. It may be a logically compelling one; it may even be true; but to whom would he make the argument? It may be that when one is alone in existence one passes the time as best one may, and that doing so may even run to philosophizing aloud, but it seems a depressingly sterile recreation.) Could anyone actually take this position as a way of being, or is it only an exercise in philosophizing? If someone were truly a solipsist, how could you tell? In his novel *Our Man in Havana*, Graham Greene let one of his characters, Dr. Hasselbacher, play at a kind of quasi-solipsism with an unsuspecting victim:

> "Pardon me," a voice whispered out of the shadows, "has this guy really won a hundred and forty thousand bucks?"
>
> "Yes, sir, I have won them," Dr. Hasselbacher said firmly before Wormold could reply. "I have won them as certainly as you exist, my almost unseen friend. You would not exist if I didn't believe you existed, nor would those dollars. I believe, therefore you are."
>
> "What do you mean I wouldn't exist?"

"You exist only in my thoughts, my friend. If I left this room..."

"You're nuts."

"Prove you exist, then."

"What do you mean, prove? Of course I exist. I've got a first-class business in real estate: a wife and a couple of kids in Miami: I flew here this morning by Delta: I'm drinking this Scotch, aren't I?" The voice contained a hint of tears.

"Poor fellow," Dr. Hasselbacher said, "you deserve a more imaginative creator than I have been. Why didn't I do better for you than Miami and real estate? Something of imagination. A name to be remembered."

"What's wrong with my name?"...

"Nothing that I cannot remedy by taking a little thought."

"You ask anyone in Miami about Harry Morgan..."

"I really should have done better than that. But I'll tell you what I'll do," Dr. Hasselbacher said, "I'll go out of the bar for a minute and eliminate you. Then I'll come back with an improved version."

"What do you mean, an improved version?"

"Now if my friend, Mr. Wormold here, had invented you, you would have been a happier man. He would have given you an Oxford education, a name like Pennyfeather..."

"What do you mean, Pennyfeather? You've been drinking."

"Of course I've been drinking. Drink blurs the imagination. That's why I thought you up in so banal a way: Miami and real estate, flying Delta. Pennyfeather would have come from Europe by K.L.M., he would be drinking his national drink, a pink gin."

"I'm drinking Scotch and I like it."

"You think you're drinking Scotch. Or rather, to be accurate, I have imagined you drinking Scotch. But we're going to change all that," Dr. Hasselbacher said cheerily. "I'll just go out in the hall for a minute and think up some real improvements."

"You can't monkey around with me," the man said with anxiety.

Dr. Hasselbacher drained his drink, laid a dollar on the bar, and rose with uncertain dignity. "You'll thank me for this," he said....

He bowed from the doorway to the agitated shadow. "I apologize for the real estate."

(I've had a good deal of fun at the expense of solipsists, if there are any. I feel obliged to say that if you are one, and you're at all offended, then you truly have only yourself to blame.)

Let's take it, then, that it is not possible to prove with geometric logic that anything exists outside our minds. Even that plural is illogical and beyond proof. My mind, then. So the fact that I am writing this in obvious hope that someone will read it suggests that I have a way out of the bind. Yes, I do; but so do we all. We all assume that there is a world out there. It is not a conscious assumption, not a choice from among competing propositions. "Let's see, do I wish to believe in the existence of a world, or shall I not? And if so, which one?" No one begins the day or life by undertaking such a process of ratiocination. From first infantile perception, the world is *there*. And it pretty much stays there. What changes is how we understand it.

The match so far: I, [your name], exist; and there is additional stuff, provisionally labeled "the world," outside me. The first clause is given me as knowledge; the second I take as necessary to any manner of life richer than self-contemplation. I am prepared to devise practical relationships with "the world."

Now, then, how do things stand as between me and it, geographically, as it were? Here once more we encounter something so common and fundamental as seldom to evoke comment. We are, each of us, the geographical center of the world. (To be quite honest, I am. About you I cannot be sure, but I will give you the benefit of the doubt, as explained below in "The higher common sense.") Turn your head, turn your whole body, and the world reveals itself as arranged radially about you. This remains true whatever orientation your body assumes and wherever in the world it moves. Everything out there is, first and foremost, to be observed in terms of "in front

58

of," "behind," "to the right of," or "to the left of," "above" or "below"...me (yes, or you).

There is a quite neat analogy between this egocentric view of the world and the geocentric view of the cosmos that many cultures have taken. The general view in ancient Greece, for example (though not a unanimous one), was that the Moon, the Sun, the five planets (those visible to the naked eye), and the stars all were fixed to spheres that were centered on the Earth and that rotated about that center, giving rise to the apparent motions of those bodies in the sky. As closer observations revealed more and more complexity in the motions of the bodies (especially the occasional apparent retrograde motions of the planets) it became necessary (at least for the meticulous Greeks) to devise more and more complex modifications to the basic model in order to accommodate the observations. Eventually the model fell of its own weight and intractability (assisted by some profound changes in how the evidence was understood). The work of Copernicus, Brahe, Galileo, Kepler, and Newton produced a model of the cosmos in which Earth is but one of many planets revolving about the Sun. The Earth is no longer the center, no longer in a unique or privileged position, but merely one body among many. Later work shifted the Sun from the center of the observed universe to the outskirts of a galaxy of some billions of citizen stars, and then revealed that galaxy as but one among countless many, and finally (in the mind experiments of Albert Einstein) demonstrated that there could in principle be no privileged or fundamental frame of reference in the cosmos.

The analogy suggests, if nothing else does, that our native egocentric view is open to criticism. Am I in any real sense the center of something more than my own consciousness? Common sense suggests, in turn, that just as it is natural to see the cosmos as centered on Earth simply because that is the vantage from which we view it, so similarly natural is the naive view that I am the center of my observed world, a view that is a direct function of my being located in one particular spot rather than in many or in none.

The match so far: I, [your name], exist; I exist in a world; and though my being a finite and located being constrains me to see that world in a certain way, that is a fact about me and not about the world.

One matter remains to be considered under this head, and the resolution will be no surprise. When the occasion arises in which some idea of mine is to be compared with or tested against an idea of another, I often find my own the stronger contender, the more convincing candidate for acceptance. This is an instant judgment that I make. I am usually not aware that any time or effort has been required to arrive at it; indeed, it seems sometimes not a process at all, for the superiority of my idea is *prima facie*, simply evident. My idea has an immediacy, a clarity, a weight that I do not find in the other. It is present in its fullness, and its implications (some of them, anyway) are laid out before me. It shines, and it feels right. It is "clear and distinct." Robust, indeed, is the idea that could displace my own, given such a head start.

Extending the analogy that we have been using, though, forces me to concede at least the possibility that these seeming virtues that attend my idea are a product of real estate – location, location, location – rather than of real value. The idea in my head has the advantage of being where it is, irrespective of its intrinsic worth, while the one from outside is available to me only through the slow and uncertain medium of language, which may be able to convey the purely rational content but lacks bandwidth to carry the multimedia effects. Or, to employ a related analogy: As I sit on my patio of an evening, the fireflies in the yard are brighter than the exploding stars somewhere in the galaxies above my head.

the higher common sense

One way of viewing the history of Western rationalism since it was inaugurated by the Greeks (as we conventionally credit them, though people were rational before the Greeks and the Greeks themselves were not in every instance all that rational; we mean that rationalism was erected into a method and a principle by certain Greek thinkers and has had a fairly successful career since then), one view of this history is of the successive displacement of the subjective by the objective. To the extent that this is true, it has proceeded cautiously, from the outside inward. First, the abandonment of the geocentric view, that Earth is at the center of the cosmos; then of the heliocentric view, that our solar system is at the center; then of the recognition that not even our galaxy, or any galaxy, is at the center and that, for physics and astronomy, at least, there is no center. Later, with the rise of psychology (first as a province of philosophy), came the realization that the particular circumstances in which one individual reaches a judgment – his unique geographic location to begin with, along with his unique set of experiences – might yield a unique yet rational judgment. In other words, to some questions there might not be a single, purely objective and universal answer.

For some philosophers these have been fightin' words. Some in the latter stretches of the long line of Rationalists have learned to claim that the lesson of psychology is simply the limited nature of the individual who is not rigorously trained to reason (*i.e.*, is not a philosopher). The true Thinker, austere and ascetic, would rise above mere circumstance, above subjectivity, above all interest, perhaps above human nature itself, to seek and ultimately behold the Truth. Popular literature has been more divided on the matter, often linking a notable power of ratiocination with a variety of peculiar, even fatal, personality traits. Sherlock Holmes with his various quirks comes to mind.

Some other philosophers have taken the opposite tack and thrown in whole hog with subjectivity. There is and can be only the individual and his partial, clouded, and mainly self-interested view of the world. All is subjectivity! All is relative! There is no truth save My Truth! This makes an attractive cloak for those preparing or apologizing for a life of dissolution, and it has produced a certain amount of charmingly decadent late Romantic poetry to be embraced by succeeding generations of adolescents, but its value as a practical guide to life is nil.

For the most part, opinion has settled somewhere in the middle, though it is a vast middle with room for apparently infinite shadings. William James, one of the more reasonable explorers of this territory, put it thus:

> Here in this room, we all of us believe in molecules and the conservation of energy, democracy and necessary progress, in Protestant Christianity and the duty of fighting for 'the doctrine of the immortal Monroe,' all for no reasons worthy of the name. We see into these matters with no more inner clearness, and probably with much less, than any disbeliever in them might possess. His unconventionality would probably have some grounds to show for its conclusions; but for us, not insight, but the *prestige* of the opinions, is what makes the spark shoot from them and light up our sleeping magazines of faith. Our reason is quite satisfied, in nine hundred and ninety-nine cases out of every thousand of us, if it can find a few arguments that will do to recite in case our credulity is criticised by some one else. Our faith is faith in some one else's faith, and in the greatest matters this is most the case. Our belief in truth itself, for

> instance, that there is a truth, and that our
> minds and it are made for each other; –
> what is it but a passionate affirmation of
> desire, in which our social system backs us
> up?

We might just dare to go a step farther than James on grounds that we considered in the last chapter. Taking a view of the human species as a product of organic evolution, we might well feel justified in inferring from its success so far in surviving, in changing for the better its average condition of life, in building tools (both physical and mental) for mastering aspects of the world beyond its original grasp, that some portion, anyway, of the opinions it has developed and employed in this program of (call it) progress are well founded, perhaps even true (whatever that means). But Mr. James might well respond that the very terms of our suggested extension of his position betray all sorts of assumptions that are little more than social conventions (though more lively ones in this age than, say, the Monroe Doctrine). He would be right, of course, but notice that he is not saying that we could or should behave otherwise. Rather he is suggesting that we might serve ourselves better by understanding, and bearing in mind, the fact that much, perhaps all, of what passes for knowledge is something other than just plain truth.

The match so far: I, [your name], exist; I exist in a world; some relationship obtains between me and that world, but it's beginning to seem less simple than I thought.

common sense justified

Let's back up a bit. In the last chapter we asked the question, "If there is knowledge in my head, how did it get there?" and we decided to believe, provisionally, that the reports of the senses about a world outside my head had something serious to do with it. What, exactly? Are those reports themselves knowledge? Are my visual impressions – those patches of color, some of them in motion – and aural impressions – sounds of various pitches and loudnesses, some of them pure and most mixed – and all the rest, are they What I Know? I don't think so. What I Know is that, for example, *this* colored patch *right here* is my dog, and *that* one over there looks like Elvis but cannot be; that the particular sound I am attending to right now is that of an oboe, while I am trying to ignore another sound, that of an airplane approaching O'Hare. I know that the increasingly annoying tactile sensation somewhat to the south of the others is caused by a chair that is poorly designed for working. I know that if I turn around there will be no one there looking over my shoulder. And so on and on...I know a great many things, mostly of no interest to anyone else. How did I get from simple sensations to these statements about the world that I call knowledge?

A simple answer, and therefore one to be suspicious of, is that I built them. A more scientific answer, and therefore one to be suspicious of, is that "knowledge" results from a complex interaction of sensory inputs with various hard-wired and learned patterns of neurological processing, leading to behaviors (including especially speech) that conform to and are continually modified by social norms and influences. Once again, psychologists, philosophers, and cognitive scientists of sundry sorts have proposed a great many differing ways to tell this story, and the time when we will be able to settle on a single accepted version is nowhere in sight. Fortunately, it need not be for our purposes.

> Knowledge is considered by most in our culture as something one discovers, not something that one makes. Knowledge is out there waiting to be found, and the most useful tool for finding it is science. If there

> were a greater appreciation for the extent to
> which knowledge is constructed – something
> made – there might be a greater likelihood
> that its aesthetic dimensions would be
> appreciated.
>
> –Elliot Eisner

There is ample evidence that we are born with some very strong inclinations to respond in certain ways to certain kinds of sensory data. Newborns, for example, seem to know what faces are almost as soon as they open their eyes. This is not to say that a newborn looking up at the nurse thinks "Ah, there's a face, so I'll smile and perhaps whoever it is will pick me up." At first it is a simple matter of stimulus: a certain pattern of visual data; and response: turning the head toward and perhaps a certain readiness to respond further, all mediated by some pattern-recognizing-and-response-triggering mechanism in the brain. The further steps of applying a label (a "face") to the sensation and thereby consciously both associating it with others of a similar sort and distinguishing it from those that are not, are abilities that develop later. Later still come such matters as perceiving causality in the world and the formation of purpose and purposive action around what has been perceived. But something, nowadays thought most likely to be some sort of neural network, permits the newborn who "knows" nothing in any conventional sense to "know" a face when he sees one. The advantage of having such a network built in is easy to see. The baby is prepared to respond to others of his kind in ways likely to support his continued existence: He will bond with parents and others, evoking their interest and assistance. Such an advantageous ability, once evolved, will tend to be conserved because the babies that have it are more likely to be fed and sheltered and eventually to grow up and reproduce than are babies who fail to respond to the presence of others.

What else do we bring into the world besides a face-identifying network? Many such abilities or faculties or instincts (as they have been labeled at one time or another), some obvious and some not so. We bring preferences for certain kinds of taste sensations over others, preferences that help us avoid eating many otherwise attractive candidate foods that are actually harmful. (There is even evidence that the perception of the facial expression associated with disgust, such as might be evoked by a bad taste or smell, is processed in a different part of the brain from those that process other emotions. The advantage of privileged processing of such information is similarly clear.) We bring a strong tendency to hang around with our own kind (a category that is continually redefined through the life of the individual). We bring a potential to develop language and a strong drive to use it. We bring a powerful capacity to detect patterns of certain kinds in our sensations and, correspondingly, to create patterns and endow them with meaning. We bring curiosity. And

> We are born believing. A man bears beliefs,
> as a tree bears apples.
> –Ralph Waldo Emerson

Many of those beliefs may never rise into our consciousness. Such is the belief that there is a world outside us; unless we are philosophically inclined, or in some other way impaired, it does not occur to us that there might be a question about it. Another such is the belief that those other people-shaped objects around us are, in fact, occupied by consciousnesses like our own. That is, we instinctively have a theory of mind that includes a theory of other minds. We don't, most of us, have to be convinced that other people are like us, even though the consciousness of another may be the most unapproachable phenomenon in the universe. It is not simply that we don't know what it is to be a bat; we don't know what it is to be someone else, however much like us the someone

66

might be. On that kind of evidence we would certainly reject, or at least hold at arm's length, any number of propositions about the rest of the world, but we seem predisposed – wired – to accept this one kind of otherness. (One reason the scene from *Our Man in Havana* is so funny is that it subverts this instinctive belief in the likeness of others to ourselves. Dr. Hasselbacher treats the helpless Morgan as we would never treat another, and Morgan's frustration perfectly captures the futility of arguing with a solipsist.)

The match so far: I, [your name], exist; I exist in a world; that world makes various impressions upon me, but I am not just a passive blank tablet to be written on.

common unsense

If it is true, as seems a reasonable first approximation, that the ability of the human mind to negotiate the world around it and, more than that, to create coherent explanations for the phenomena it observes, rests on a fundamental proclivity to detect and to create patterns, it would be prudent to understand as much as we can of the nature and, especially, the limitations of that faculty. Certainly we encounter patterns almost everywhere, and where we do not encounter them we impose them. The objects of which we see the world to be composed are patterns of visual and other sensations; our behavior is to a very large extent composed of reflex, habit, and learned response, all of which can be understood as patterns of various provenances; our deep response to physical and sonic rhythms, and our parallel inclination to make them, underlies our music, our games, our social life generally. We understand our art in terms of pattern, whether it be music, painting, literature, or theatre.

All of this is quite reasonable in a universe characterized by, so far as we can detect, regular physical processes that produce regular, *i.e.*, patterned, signals to which the likes of us can learn to respond usefully. In that sort of universe, beings who are the product of organic evolution might be expected to have developed some number of variations on a basic ability to detect and create patterns. By the same token, it might be expected that there would be limits to this pattern-detecting ability as a tool for understanding the deeper structure of that universe, its workings at levels that do not bear directly upon the questions of survival and reproduction.

Much of what goes by the name of "common sense" for most people is a store of learned-but-now-largely-unconscious understanding of how the world works. For large ranges of everyday phenomena, we just "know" how things are and how they will develop over short times. We "know" these things because our learned responses are right often enough that we almost never have occasion to question them, that is, to raise them to the level of consciousness for inspection. We see the ball hit by the bat, and within milliseconds we "know" where to run and how to position our hands to catch the ball. (How we do this, we do not know. Formally, the feat is equivalent to solving some simultaneous differential equations, something most people cannot consciously do at all, and certainly not in time to make the out. Machines capable of doing it in real time, that is, in time to actually permit the ball to be caught, have been around for only a few decades, and even now they cannot do the whole trick.) We drop a glass of milk and are irked, but unsurprised, that a cleanup job results. A gale of wind pushes against us as we walk and we automatically lean into it.

On the other hand, there are kinds of pattern that we are not only not wired to detect and process but which we have, most of us, great difficulty quite grasping even when they are taught to us. A prime example is statistical pattern. We have no instinct for statistics whatever, which is why Las Vegas is rich and you and I are not. If we flip a coin and get ten tails in a row we believe that heads is more likely to turn up on the next flip, and even when we "know" better we often catch ourselves believing against what we know. We feel that a batter who has gone 0-for-20 is "due" for a hit, and when he eventually does hit the ball we are pleased to have been right. In part this disability of ours is a consequence of our pattern-detecting ability, which sometimes can lead us to infer patterns, to assume connections, where there are none, or to use patterns that apply in one domain to another in which they are quite inappropriate.

Much effort has been expended by psychologists to understand how we learn these elements of "common sense" and incorporate them into our unconscious strategy for daily living. We do not know how astonished we ought to be at living in a universe that is so regular-seeming as to permit this kind of strategy. It is impossible to imagine life in a universe with no or little regularity, such that virtually every situation, every moment, is or has to be considered potentially unique. Without the luxury of habitual behavior, which includes learned interpretations of our sensations, we should at the very least be utterly exhausted from the effort.

How curious it is, then, that the endeavor that is arguably one of our chief claims to consideration as a species uses that very pattern-detecting and -making ability seemingly to undermine so much of our "common sense." That endeavor is science, the systematic attempt to create a rational, coherent, and verifiable account of the world around us. The scientific method is all about pattern: Take a batch of observations and try to find patterns in them; then create a higher-level pattern, called a hypothesis, that would, if true, entail the patterns observed; from that higher-level pattern, infer some pattern that has not yet been observed; institute some process to attempt to observe the inferred pattern; if the inferred pattern is observed, elevate the hypothesis to the status of theory, and proceed to use the theory until either (a) some observations seem to contradict it, or (b) an alternative hypothesis with additional predictive power or simpler structure is proposed.

Note that the scientific method, far from being magic or even esoteric, is simply a conscious and systematic application of what we all do under the heading of "common sense." Because the scientist does it consciously, he does not settle immediately for the first likely solution that occurs to him but subjects it to various tests; and because he does it systematically, he tries every way he can think of to disprove his solution before at last accepting it. As contrasted with everyday methods, this saves many a bump.

(Note, too, that the word "truth" does not appear in the foregoing explanation of the scientific method, nor do any of its usual synonyms or proxies. We look for patterns with explanatory and predictive powers. Often there may be more than one candidate pattern. If they seem to be of equal explanatory and predictive capacity, then our rule of thumb is Occam's Razor: we pick the simplest one. Being the simplest one does not guarantee that it is "true," only that it is economical.)

Armed with this powerful method, humans have attained a degree of understanding of and control over the world that amazes even ourselves. The power of the method is most vividly illustrated by its ability to produce rational, coherent, verifiable accounts of aspects of the world that contradict the "common sense" with which we began. George Gamow taught many a would-be scientist decades ago the amazing fact that it is quite possible, in terms of physical law, for the water in a glass suddenly to fly upward toward the ceiling. Our "common sense" knowledge that gravity keeps it in place, or, as we might have thought before "gravity" became an element of "common sense," that things just sit there unless disturbed, turns out to be a matter of statistics rather than law. The water consists of some extremely large, but finite, number of molecules, each moving at some velocity and bouncing regularly off others. Their individual motions are beyond our ability to track or calculate, or any conceivable mechanism of tracking or calculating, so only statistical representations of the collective motion are possible. Among the uncountable possible configurations of this mass of molecules, each of which is equally probable and possible, is one in which they are all moving at the same instant in the same direction, namely up. If that were actually to occur, we should see the mass of water fly upward out of the glass. As Gamow proceeded to show, the chance of this happening, rather than one of the overwhelming number of configurations that involve the water, as a mass, staying where it appears to be, is so small that we would almost certainly have to wait longer than the expected lifetime of the universe to see it. But, then, it might happen tomorrow.

This is a simple, though disturbing, example of how the real nature of the world, as we have been able to determine it, differs radically from our "common sense" view. We've been trained, individually and as a culture, on the everyday, the probable, the middle-sized. When we begin to examine the very large, as in the universe as a whole, or the very small, as at the quantum level, our expectations fail. We have no means to grasp what is apparently going on. We may recoil from the implications of our own reasoning, as Albert Einstein did from some implications of quantum theory. Our most deeply held beliefs about how the world works are called into question or simply violated.

An even more bizarre – I beg your pardon, *counterintuitive* (a much more professional adjective) – example is the well known two-slit experiment. In this experiment, usually performed not with real equipment but simply as a thought-experiment, electrons from some source are directed toward a barrier in which there are two slits. Some distance behind the barrier is a screen along which can be moved a detector that responds when an electron strikes. The experiment consists of noting how many electrons strike at successive points along the screen and inferring how many have passed through each slit. I will not explain it further here (many books on modern physics do it better than I could) but will quickly jump to the upshot, which is that electrons do not behave entirely like separate, distinguishable particles nor entirely like waves but a little like each. One of the paradoxical results of the experiment is that the pattern of electron strikes at the screen differs according to whether I am watching the electrons or not. It can be shown to be in principle impossible to predict how any particular electron will behave. That is, given no matter how much information about the electron beforehand, we cannot say whether it will pass through the one slit or the other. While in our midrange everyday world we know that a moving object will get from Point A to Point B by way of a straight line (more or less; gravity or wind or some other external force may modify the actual path a bit), it has become the working method of quantum physics to assume that any path is possible and instead of assuming one to calculate instead the various probabilities associated with all paths.

Richard Feynman described the situation in this way:

> When people say that nature must have causality, you can use Newton's law; or if they say that nature must be stated in terms of a minimum principle, you talk about it this last way; or if they insist that nature must have a local field – sure, you can do that. The question is: which one is right?...One of the amazing characteristics of nature is the variety of interpretational schemes which is possible....
>
> Now we know how the electrons and light behave. But what can I call it? If I say they behave like particles I give the wrong

impression; also if I say they behave like waves....They behave in a way that is like nothing that you have ever seen before. Your experience with things that you have seen before is incomplete....But the difficulty really is psychological and exists in the perpetual torment that results from your saying to yourself, "But how can it be like that?" Which is a reflection of uncontrolled but utterly vain desire to see it in terms of something familiar....There was a time when the newspapers said that only twelve men understood the theory of relativity. I do not believe there ever was such a time. There might have been a time when only one man did, because he was the only guy who caught on, before he wrote his paper. But after people read the paper a lot of people understood the theory of relativity in some way or other, certainly more than twelve. On the other hand, I think I can safely say that nobody understands quantum mechanics....I am going to tell you what nature behaves like. If you will simply admit that maybe she does behave like this, you will find her a delightful, entrancing thing. Do not keep saying to yourself, if you can possibly avoid it, "But how can it be like that?" because you will get "down the drain," into a blind alley from which nobody has yet escaped. Nobody knows how it can be like that.

Physicists, like the rest of us, have grown up in a world where there are particles and there are waves, and each provides a useful model for understanding certain other phenomena. But when they began to study in detail the behavior of electrons and photons, the models failed. What we commonly say is that electrons behave sometimes like particles and sometimes like waves. But this does not mean that they are particles that occasionally act weird, nor that they are waves that occasionally act weird. It is much more likely the case that they simply behave like electrons, but we don't have any model available that would permit us to grasp what that means. Physicists take the trouble to train themselves to think like electrons, as it were; they expend considerable effort to make themselves some new intuitions simply so that they can get on with their work.

Infants do not have the ability to catch a fly ball. Rather, they are equipped in some way to learn how to do that. It is a little too misleading to use some such metaphor as that "the machinery is in place" or "the brain is prewired," but somehow the brain is ready, and the practice that will realize this potential begins as soon as the infant is old enough to begin noticing what happens to objects when they are released from the grasp. (Even that apparently simple step is built on many prior ones, like learning to recognize objects-that-are-not-oneself and learning to work the hand and arm muscles and learning to coordinate muscular modulations with visual data, and so on and on.) The knowledge that things fall when released and move in certain other ways when propelled, is actively created, built over time into the brain and perhaps into the muscles themselves. It is preverbal knowledge and does not become a matter of conscious thought for a long time. Until then, and for almost all the time after that as well, it is simply the way world as we know it is. (The fascination of balloons for children surely lies in their gently violating this law. Later, too, we learn that balloons are not magic, and the reasons for this exception are also incorporated into our world-knowledge.) This kind of knowledge becomes so firmly seated and is so easily relied on precisely because it works almost all the time. Contrary understanding, such as we may gain from scientific investigation, does not abolish it. Thus we learn to expect undisturbed things to just lie there; later we learn that this is, in some cases, a matter of statistics rather than law; but our expectations remain the same.

Humans have constructed tools of thought by which they are able to extend their understanding into realms that the brain, as a simple product of evolution, is not necessarily suited to probing. In quantum physics, and perhaps in cognitive science, we may be pressing against some real limits to our ability to understand, or perhaps rather against some limitations in our idea of what "understanding" means.

The match so far: I, [your name], exist; I exist in a world that I seem to be able to make some sense of, most of the time, up to a point.

all-too-common nonsense

Ideologies, whether in-built patterns of processing or grand programs for the reorganization of society, constitute the world as we experience it. Without them we would have no conscious life at all. Layer upon layer of interpretive processing render bare sense impressions into a textured world of recognizable objects and meaningful relations. The interpretive structures I bring to bear determine what I see of the world, what its facts are, what things even count as facts. That an apple is red is a product of one of my in-built interpretive patterns. The apple itself simply reflects light of certain frequencies; only in my consciousness is there red. Red is how my neural networks represent a certain pattern of stimulation, and so far as I know it has no innate significance beyond the fact that it is distinguishable from blue, green, yellow, and so on. By the same token, the limitations of my inner interpretive mechanisms may make it difficult, even impossible, to see or make sense of data that does not fit with my experience.

Galileo had great difficulty persuading some of his critics that he had observed through his telescope dark spots upon the Sun. The critics dismissed his report because they knew already that the Sun, being a celestial object and therefore perfect, could not show such blemishes. Galileo was obliged to argue thus:

> It proves nothing to say...that it is
> unbelievable for dark spots to exist in the
> sun because the sun is a most lucid body. So
> long as men were in fact obliged to call the
> sun "most pure and most lucid," no shadows
> or impurities whatever had been perceived in
> it; but now it shows itself to us as partly
> impure and spotty, why should we not call it
> "spotted and not pure"? For names and
> attributes must be accommodated to the
> essence of things, and not the essence to
> the names, since things come first and
> names afterwards.

It is time to look briefly at ideologies of the Big-I sort. These are programs of belief that purport to explain how the world really is – the hidden reality behind the appearances that mislead the unenlightened – and, more often than not, how it ought to be. Here "the world" means mainly those upper levels of social, political, and economic arrangements that obtain among humans, not the lower levels of physics and chemistry. These programs are not usually presented as belief systems, however, but as truth systems. Unlike science, which looks for the best available explanation – where "best" means both the ability to fit past observations into a coherent framework and the ability to predict further observations – and is ready to drop any explanation in favor of a better one, Ideologies purport to present final truths. They do not admit to being provisional in any way. They are based, as Isaiah Berlin wrote, on "one unchanging, all-embracing, sometimes self-contradictory and incomplete, at times fanatical, unitary inner vision." Sometimes they are discovered or built by the use of reason, and sometimes they are the stuff of revelation, but in either case they are given to the rest of us as simply true.

Ideologies may be built upon very elaborate intellectual structures, but they are usually promoted in the form of fairly simple statements. There are two reasons for this. One is that ideologies are typically in search of adherents, of believers, and recruiting is made easier by the use of slogans. The other is that ideologies are almost always simplifying in purpose. They propose quite simple explanations for the immensely complex phenomena of the world we live in. For that reason their characteristic propositions tend to equate complexity with some single, simple quality: "All of everything is simply x." History offers innumerable examples.

All things are one.

In the beginning was the Word.

We hold these truths to be self-evident, that all men are created equal....

The history of all hitherto existing society is the history of class struggles.

Contemporary science definitely confirms that the fundamental condition of our existence is to revolve.

Love makes the world go 'round.

Each offers a pattern of explanation, and most go on to derive a system of implications that involves belief, a frame of interpretation, and perhaps a way of life. Most of us accept to some degree one or more of the extant ideologies of this kind, for they make up much of the web of relations we call society. They place us in our time, our culture, our neighborhood. They constitute a final layer, as it were, in our cognitive machinery, the layer whose output is that part of our daily life that lies above the merely mechanical.

The match so far: I, [your name], exist; I exist in a world that I seem to be able to make some sense of, most of the time, up to a point; and that fact doesn't entirely satisfy me.

living with ideologies

A generation of Americans once grew up with the belief that the last word in hard-headed realism and gimlet-eyed skepticism (to say nothing of clench-jawed determination) was

"Just the facts, ma'am."

It is probably no fault of Jack Webb's that they also generally thought of "facts" as though they were the hard, determinate, self-explanatory things – a sort of truth marbles – that Sgt. Friday was forever seeking to sift out of the ramblings of his interviewees. Most of us think that way. "Facts are facts," goes the old saying, and we are under the impression that we have said something when we say it. We think of facts as though they were actually there, and we think of making a case or a proof as a matter of reaching into a sack and selecting just the right combination of facts to be arranged.

As even Sgt. Friday must have known, however, if facts were like that there would be no need for trials ever to have been held in and for the county of Los Angeles. The facts do not speak for themselves because they aren't there. What is there is a world, as perceived through the medium of the senses and as constructed *by* us through the application of layers of selection, pattern-matching, and extrapolation. Selection may

78

be passive (as when we don't hear ourselves breathing when we're listening to music or a conversation) or active (as when we are attempting to find an explanation for some phenomenon), but it always involves filtering out from the mass of impressions we take in every instant those few that we have decided are salient, that bear upon the matter in question. But the decision about what is salient must be based on something, for it is not simply random, nor are aspects of the world labeled and classified for our convenience. The something may be what we call experience or it may be what we call inference or it may be something else altogether, but the choice of this filter or that one is an assumption that by this means we will narrow the field down to an appropriate subset of aspects or features that really have to do with our present interest. And as our attention, our intentions, our moods, our situation changes from moment to moment, so too does the filter and consequently the content and texture of the world it allows to pass through to our consciousness.

The upshot is simply this: It's interpretation all the way down. From the explicit Ideologies that teach us to see, for example, relations between individuals in terms of struggling social classes or alternatively in terms of love, all the way back to the neural wiring that conditions us to see those individuals not as colored patches or as large bipedal , self-moving objects cluttering the space around us but as persons like ourselves, with similar internal lives – we live in an intelligible world by virtue of layer upon layer of interpretation. We have no idea whatever what the world would look like without those filters, and most likely the very suggestion is without real meaning.

The match so far: deuce.

5: evidence and authority

> Alice laughed. "There's no use trying," she
> said: "one *can't* believe impossible things."
> "I daresay you haven't had much practice,"
> said the Queen. "When I was your age, I
> always did it for half-an-hour a day. Why,
> sometimes I've believed as many as six
> impossible things before breakfast."
> —Lewis Carroll

Let's think back to the cocktail-party scene we imagined in
Chapter 2 and recapture, if we can, something of the
excitement of the moment. My opponent and I were "trading
fours," as they say in jazz argot. He'd play a fact and I would
try to match or top it; then he would play another, more
obscure, one, and so on. (I'm resisting the temptation to
compare this scene with that Western-movie cliché in which
the ambitious young hothead tries to provoke the retired
gunfighter in order to establish an instant reputation.
Resisting, but apparently not hard enough.) Now try to
imagine that you are among the onlookers at this contest and,
further (stretch yourself), that the topic – it was the War of
Jenkins' Ear, you'll recall, but it could be anything from
abalone to zymurgy – actually interests you. Because it does,
some of the facts tossed into play are likely to stick to your
brain. "West Indies, eh? And Spain. I'll have to remember
that," you perhaps think to yourself. You leave the party some
time later feeling enriched, possibly among other effects. It
may be that your motive is the purest curiosity about the wars
of colonial America or some such thing; or, as we suggested
earlier, it may be that this is a cheap way to collect trivia to
use in some future contest of your own. In either case, one
simple fact underlies your deciding to store up these bits of

knowledge: You bought it. You have accepted what you heard at face value. Why?

Here's another story, this time a true one. One day while wandering not entirely aimlessly around the World Wide Web, I came upon a page that was intended to induce me to subscribe to a newsletter published by a political organization of some sort. The inducement consisted of the argument that the news reported by the "corporate media," as they were referred to, meaning the wire services and most newspapers and all television, is slanted or even censored to fit corporate interests. This is not a particularly original view, and mild versions of it have been held by quite reasonable people. (The complementary view is that they are in the clutches of some radical political obsession. This view, too, is arguable.) To clinch the case against the mainstream media, the writer of this advertisement included this revelation:

> Fortunately, at least one highly-respected journalist has publicly confessed that this is indeed the case. Asked to give a toast before the prestigious New York Press Club in 1953, John Swinton, the former Chief of Staff at the NEW YORK TIMES, made this candid confession [it's worth noting that Swinton was called "The Dean of His Profession" by other newsmen, who admired him greatly]:
>
> "There is no such thing, at this date of the world's history, as an independent press. You know it and I know it. There is not one of you who dares to write your honest opinions, and if you did, you know beforehand that it would never appear in print. I am paid weekly for keeping my honest opinions out of the paper I am connected with. Others of you are paid

similar salaries for similar things, and any of
you who would be so foolish as to write
honest opinions would be out on the streets
looking for another job.

"If I allowed my honest opinions to appear in
one issue of my paper, before twenty-four
hours my occupation would be gone. The
business of the journalist is to destroy the
truth; to lie outright; to pervert; to vilify; to
fawn at the feet of mammon, and to sell the
country for his daily bread. You know it and I
know it and what folly is this toasting an
independent press. We are the tools and
vassals of the rich men behind the scenes.
We are the jumping jacks, they pull the
strings and we dance. Our talents, our
possibilities and our lives are all the property
of other men. We are intellectual
prostitutes."

A powerful, indeed damning, statement, that, and it is easy to
see why someone promoting an alternative source of news
would find it useful to repeat it. I found it interesting enough to
look around a bit more, and I found this same quotation from
John Swinton cited in dozens of Web sites and in online
discussions. In something called the ISCNI Flash 1.20, under
the heading "DON'T BELIEVE EVERYTHING YOU READ IN THE
NEWSPAPER," I found it introduced by these comments:

Admittedly, this statement makes no
mention of UFOs, and Swinton probably
wasn't thinking of UFOs when he made it –
more likely, he was thinking of how badly
the national press in 1953 was intimidated
by the likes of Senator Joe McCarthy – but it
applies, then and now, to any subject about

which the government or other powerful
interests wish to control public opinion.

(It turns out that ISCNI stands for the International Society for
Contact with Non-human Intelligence, an organization
apparently devoted to telling various *X-Files*ish truths that
have been suppressed by this or that secret arm of the
government.) The ISCNI editor is right about one thing: John
Swinton was probably not thinking about UFOs. On the other
hand, he certainly wasn't thinking about Joe McCarthy, either.
That is because in 1953 Swinton was speaking to no one; he
had died in 1901.

Something about the language of the quote made me wonder,
so I did a little elementary library research. Swinton was a
journalist, to be sure, and a well respected one. It is also true
that he was chief of the editorial staff of the *New York Times*
for ten years, though the years were 1860 to 1870. Later he
published his own newspaper for a time. He was a political
activist, a friend or admirer of such radical reformers as Emma
Goldman and Karl Marx. He was especially noted for his
brilliance in invective and sarcasm, his mastery of the
"language of opprobrium," as the biographical sketch I read
put it.

The mistake here is not simply in getting the date wrong, as by
a simple typographical error. Assuming for the moment that
Swinton did say what is attributed to him, and I think it quite
likely he did (although none of the Web sites I looked at gave a
source for the quote, an online critic later pointed me to *The
Brass Check*, a critique of American journalism published by
Upton Sinclair in 1919), the context in which he said it must be
taken into account. He became a journalist at a time when
there was little professional about that line of work, when
newspaper publishers and editors battled for circulation and
advertising by means that today would be unthinkable (well,
except by the supermarket tabloids, who are following in a

long-established, if not particularly admirable, tradition). In April 1844, for example, when Swinton was 14 years old, a sensational story in the New York *Sun* caused an enormous crowd to gather in the streets around the paper's offices to await more news. The story? It was, supposedly, a three-day crossing of the Atlantic Ocean by balloon, a feat described by the journalist who wrote the original story as "unquestionably the most stupendous, the most interesting, and the most important undertaking ever accomplished or even attempted by man." The journalist was Edgar Allan Poe, better known to later ages for tales that were acknowledged to be fiction. The publication of the "Balloon-Hoax" is notable only for the identity of the journalist, for it was altogether characteristic of journalism in that time. The *Sun*'s circulation did jump substantially as a result.

Some of the sites that offer up Swinton's comments as inside proof that the mainstream media are not to be trusted further bolster his authority by reminding us that the *New York Times* takes as its motto "All the News That's Fit to Print." When Swinton was associated with the *Times*, however, it was a small, struggling upstart no better than its peers, and that motto was not adopted until decades later, in 1896, when it was still more hopeful than descriptive. That was the period when another newspaper, William Randolph Hearst's *New York Journal*, used all its ingenuity, including for false reporting, to drum up a war with Spain.

One begins to see, then, that shifting the quote from most likely sometime in the 1880s to 1953 makes a great difference in how it is to be understood; and failing to identify the author as a political radical who struggled for a few years to publish his own newspaper in competition with the larger establishment journals clouds our understanding further. Interesting, isn't it, how these antiestablishment publications expect us to accept their versions of the truth solely on the basis of their own claims about the biases of the mainstream press, claims bolstered by an essentially bogus anecdote?

One more thing: Notice that in the quote what Swinton claims is being suppressed, what he and his oppressed colleagues would be fired for printing, is his "honest opinion." Not the news, not the truth, whatever those may be; opinion.

It's too easy to poke holes in much of what is published on the Web, or said in newsgroups, or hawked on talk radio. What is more interesting is thinking about how attractive the misuse of information seems to be, and how often the misuse parades under color of the "real truth" in opposition to the lies put about by some conspiracy of bankers, government, the media, the Trilateral Commission, anarchoglobalists, the pope, the Illuminati, the Masons, or aliens from Dimension X.

(In case you are not yet cured of Pierre Salinger's disease, here is an extract from yet another Web site:

> The Germans landed on the Moon as early as probably 1942, utilizing their larger exoatmospheric rocket saucers of the Miethe and Schriever type. The Miethe rocket craft was built in diameters of 15 and 50 meters, and the Schriever Walter turbine powered craft was designed as an interplanetary exploration vehicle. It had a diameter of 60 meters, had 10 stories of crew compartments, and stood 45 meters high....
>
> Everything that NASA has told the world about the Moon is a lie and it was done to keep the exclusivity of the club from joinings by the third world countries....Ever since their first day of landing on the Moon, the

Germans started boring and tunneling under
the surface and by the end of the war there
was a small Nazi research base on the Moon.

The free energy tachyon drive craft of the
Haunibu-1 and 2 type were used after 1944
to haul people, materiel and the first robots
to the construction site on the Moon. When
Russians and Americans secretly landed
together on the Moon in the early fifties with
their own saucers, they spent their first night
there as guests of the Nazis in thier [sic]
underground base.

You have to admire the skill with which the regular media
manage to hide things like this, don't you?)

Why do some people accept this sort of thing as the truth?
Why did you (I'm betting) accept my facts about the War of
Jenkins' Ear? Why are we sometimes so eager to know
something, so quick to claim knowledge, when we haven't
worked to earn it?

There seem to be only two kinds of justification on which we
rest our knowing, evidence and authority. We appeal to
evidence when we conclude from our own experience that the
world is so, that the facts are these. We appeal to authority
most of the rest of the time, anchoring ourselves to some
person, book, institution, custom. Sometimes we mix the two
and call the signs of authority by the name of "evidence."

How is evidence to be gathered, evaluated, weighed? And even
before we ask those questions, we must ask, What is to count
as evidence?

how to know

> Some circumstantial evidence is very strong,
> as when you find a trout in the milk.
> –Henry David Thoreau

I had been familiar with that quip for years before I understood it. I knew from the first that the joke lay in the sheer obviousness of a trout in milk, but what I didn't know that I didn't know was what the trout was evidence *of*. Only later did I learn that in the days before public regulation of such things, it was the practice of unscrupulous dairymen to water the milk, to add volume cheaply in order to increase their revenue and profit. Water, fish, circumstantial evidence -- you get it.

And, indeed, is *anything* to count as evidence?

> But it's the truth even if it didn't happen.
> –Ken Kesey

"I saw it with my own eyes," we sometimes argue, or maybe "It happened to me." That is good enough reason to accept something as fact and to proceed satisfied that we know whatever it is. The evidence of the senses becomes, in retrospect and suitably construed, the evidence of our experience. This is how we learn, from earliest infancy, and as we have seen, the process works pretty well, the principal evidence for which conclusion is the very fact that we are still here to talk about it. What changes from infancy forward is the kinds of construing we do and the variety of evidence on which we draw. The construing becomes increasingly sophisticated, depending on chains of inference that grow longer and longer and collections of evidence whose more complex relationships are built on previous results. It is no surprise that error is possible as things get complicated. But there's a bit of a problem lurking right at the bottom of the process, too.

A commonsensical definition of "evidence" will certainly involve some notion of relatedness: the matter that is supposed to be evidence of, for, or against x must be shown or assumed to be related in some real way to x. You may suggest to me that we plan our picnic for tomorrow because the weather forecast on television calls for a warm, sunny day. To which I reply "No. I find that I have in my pocket a quarter, a dime, and two pennies. Thirty-seven cents is a sure sign of rain."

Let's imagine that you do not immediately forget about the picnic in order to telephone for medical assistance, but instead choose to debate the question. You say "The weather forecast is based on reliable reports of actual weather conditions in various places, together with experience-tested methods for extrapolating the movement and development of fronts, air masses, and so on. It doesn't work perfectly, to be sure, but it is the best method available."

And I reply "My method never fails. I have observed that every time I have thirty-seven cents in my pocket, rain follows."

"But what possible connection can there be between the amount of change in your pocket and the weather?" you demand.

To which I answer blandly "I have no idea."

The absurdity of my position is only slightly ameliorated if I call your attention to the work of David Hume, who found that he could not demonstrate any relationship between cause and effect. He did not deny that there is a relationship – as he reported, he gladly turned from philosophizing to his billiard game in the full expectation that the balls would behave in the accustomed manner. But he pointed out that the attempt to find a rational, *a priori* basis for expecting the effect to result always from the cause inevitably led to begging the question:

Such expectation is founded on the assumption that the future will be much like the past, when we underwent the experiences that formed and shaped our expectations. A has always, in our experience, been followed by B; there never has been an instance of A not so followed, nor have we ever seen B without first having seen A. We then begin to expect B when we see A, and moreover we begin to think of A as causing B. Sometimes this "causation" seems quite clear and distinct, as in the case of one billiard ball striking another and setting it into motion. (Notice that our very language tends to assume causation; it is very awkward to say instead "one billiard ball coming into adjacency with another, followed by the second ball's commencing to move.") Sometimes the "causation" may be mediated through a chain of intervening events. And sometimes we are forced to admit that we cannot actually find a connection at all, so that our inference of causation is in fact a case of the logical error known as *post hoc ergo propter hoc* – "after that, therefore because of that."

But Hume said that not even in a case like that of the billiard balls can rational analysis discover the mechanism, the logical explanation, that links the two phenomena. We cannot truly explain how A "causes" B. "We have no idea of this connexion, nor even any distinct notion what it is we desire to know, when we endeavour at a conception of it." It's more than a little disturbing when you think of it, which is perhaps why we don't. Most interesting is the explanation that Hume found for this failure of reason, if that is what it is.

> I shall add, for a further confirmation of the foregoing theory, that, as this operation of the mind, by which we infer like effects from causes, and *vice versa*, is so essential to the subsistence of all human creatures, it is not probable that it could be trusted to the fallacious deductions of our reason, which is slow in its operations; appears not, in any

degree, during the first years of infancy; and at best is, in every age and period of human life, extremely liable to error and mistake. It is more conformable to the ordinary wisdom of nature to secure so necessary an act of the mind, by some instinct or mechanical tendency, which may be infallible in its operations, may discover itself at the first appearance of life and thought, and may be independent of all the laboured deductions of the understanding. As nature has taught us the use of our limbs, without giving us the knowledge of the muscles and nerves, by which they are activated; so has she implanted in us an instinct, which carries forward the thought in a correspondent course to that which she has established among external objects; though we are ignorant of those powers and forces, on which this regular course and succession of objects totally depends.

Reading this paragraph from our contemporary perspective, which requires among other things that we set aside the somewhat personified references to "nature" and read them instead as references to Darwinian evolution, it is hard not to see in it an anticipation of the idea of hard-wired modules in the brain dedicated to certain kinds of information processing. Some matters, Hume recognized, are too important to be left to mere reason, things like catching food and avoiding being caught.

Today, 250 years after Hume's *Enquiry Concerning Human Understanding*, we find lawyers challenging the link between cigarette smoking and cancer on the ground that medical doctors cannot specify precisely the mechanism by which the one produces the other. This does not mean that the lawyers are good philosophers, for they ignore Hume's distinction between what is appropriate in a philosophical inquiry and what is appropriate to life, in which, quite sensibly, "From causes which appear similar we expect similar effects."

Hume's investigation into the meaning of causation is in one sense rather like Descartes' into existence. In each case, the effect is more to illustrate the inadequacy of ratiocination than to reveal any deep error in our commonsense view of things. Not that there are no such errors. Recall the water on the road, and the water in the glass. Which brings us to another question: How far down do we go in trying to ground our experience, to find, or ordain, the basis on which we will build some sort of knowledge?

Hume's comments remind us that one of the strongest forms of evidence derives its very force from the fact that we usually aren't even aware of it as evidence, and it thus escapes scrutiny unless we take extraordinary measures. This is the common sense or world-knowledge we looked at in the last chapter and of which our sense of causation is an example. In situations that turn on some point of "how the world is" as we have come to know it, or on higher-level knowledge that we have fitted to that same model, it just *is so*. Ordinarily we do not even consider this a form of knowing. Doubts do not arise unless provoked, and usually it takes a deal of provoking.

> If a blind man were to ask me "Have you got two hands?" I should not make sure by looking. If I were to have any doubt of it, then I don't know why I should trust my eyes. For why shouldn't I test my eyes by looking to find out whether I see my two hands? What is to be tested by what?
> —Ludwig Wittgenstein

So we fall back on "seeing is believing" it would seem, and hoping for the best. But what of knowing? Are we forced to say that "knowing is merely believing"?

> Objective evidence and certitude are
> doubtless very fine ideals to play with, but
> where on this moonlit and dream-visited
> planet are they found?
> —William James

What about authority, then? Much of what we know, or behave as though we know, we have taken on authority. Simply put, we take it on authority when we are satisfied because so-and-so said so. So-and-so may be a teacher, a book, a political leader, a tradition, a revelation, the "media" (as we used to say, "It was in all the papers"), a talking horse. Authority may be claimed or assumed or imputed. Wherever we find it, or put it, there we can rest easy; consequently, whenever we wish to rest easy, we are apt to begin finding some authority somewhere.

We assume and expect authority whenever we ask a question: How high is Mount Everest? Why does bread rise? Where is Knob Noster? How shall we live? Who wrote the Book of Love? (Some questions, like the last, are rhetorical only, and we don't really expect an answer; we just wonder, wonder who?) When we ask a question, three things can happen. We get a correct answer; we get an incorrect answer; or we get no answer or an unintelligible one. Woody Hayes famously explained that he didn't like his football teams to use the forward pass because when you throw the ball, three things can happen and two of them are bad. The situation with questions is even worse. Of the three things that can happen, two are bad, and one of those pretends to be a good thing. Hence the great rule of thumb in judging authority: *Caveat emptor*, Let the buyer beware!

Buyer?

It is interesting that a common expression used to mark that someone has accepted a statement on authority is this: He bought it. We may press someone on what seems to us a too-ready acceptance of authority: Do you really buy that? The metaphor of exchange seems odd at first blush, but it is enlightening. No money changes hands, but there is surely a transaction. I'll defer discussing what it is that is exchanged for what to the next chapter, except to say that the information – the answer to the question – is not one of those whats but rather is the medium of exchange. This is not to say that the information that is passed along is incidental or fungible, necessarily, but simply that it is not the only value involved nor even always the principal one.

Why do we rely on authorities? Because they are, after all, authorities. And what makes them authorities? Among other things, the fact that we rely on them. Of course, they must sometimes pass other tests as well, but there is an astonishing amount of circularity in the relationship. (Every year, marking what event or season I do not know, one hears on a "news" program on television that someone called Mr. Blackwell has announced the names of the worst-dressed persons of whom he is aware. This Blackwell is referred to as an authority. Why? Apparently because that is simply what he is and how he has been referred to frequently before. He's an authority (on what, one can only guess) because he is so often cited as an authority. QED. When we wonder how some particular authority first attained that dignity, however, we immediately notice that – if we are correct in holding that knowledge, or even just the warrant of knowledge, comes either from experience or authority – the authority must have got it from one of those two sources. If from experience, then Hume's worries confront us as before; if from some other, prior authority, then we are simply moved back a generation to the same question once again. The only other possibility is revelation, and that is something I have no authority to discuss. I don't have revelations myself, nor do I know anyone who does. It does seem to me, though, that revelation must be unique among sources or warrants of knowledge in that it is not open to challenge. It is very hard to imagine someone receiving a revelation and then wondering if it is true. The very fact of it is its own warrant. If there were reason to doubt what was imparted, then the doubt would extend to its being a revelation at all. Of course, this prima facie validity only weighs with the direct recipient. For the rest of us, the reports of that recipient are of exactly the same status as those of any other authority.

Thus, if we ask our primary authority, let us call him Authority Zeke, what is the basis of his authority (generally, or with respect to a particular question), he may say "Revelation," in which case we have investigated as far as we can and must decide on our own what to make of his claim. If he doesn't say that, he may say "I saw it [or otherwise had first-hand experience]," in which case we may ask for details of his observations and examine his construal of what he saw, all the while bearing in mind the kinds of errors to which experience and the interpretation of experience are liable. If he doesn't say either of those things, he's left only to say "I had it from Authority Yolanda." We may then begin the process over again with Yolanda, who may refer us to Authority Xavier, thence to Authority Wilhelmina, Authority Victor, Ursula, Tiberias, and so on back to some authority who finally appeals to experience or to revelation. (Actually, there is one more possibility. One of them along the line may confess "I made it up" or "I heard it through the grapevine." That would be to relinquish the claim to authority, however, and in fact we would be quite surprised by such an admission.)

In this illustration I speak of authorities as though they were persons, but they need not be. They might be institutions, or traditions, or books. I have myself seen how successive generations of reference books may faithfully transmit an error, sometimes even a simple typographical error, by uncritical repetition.

Revelation aside, what we are left to conclude is that, in any given case, authority may be wrong. Therefore, if we rely on authority in that case, we will be wrong, too. Of course, we all knew this already. Indeed, we sometimes take considerable pleasure in catching authority out or in seeing it embarrassed publicly by error. It makes one wonder how they survive, these authorities. But somehow they do; and for some reason we keep coming back to appeal to them. Why is that?

Authorities differ not merely in form but in behavior. Some are content simply to sit quietly and wait to be consulted. Books are like this (they have little choice in the matter), as are the more critically self-aware – that is to say, humble – human authorities. Others like to force themselves on us. Still others are used as tools – heavy, blunt ones, typically – by third parties with ulterior motives. In this spirit, there was once something called Science, with the capital "s," appealed to by reformers and revolutionaries of one sort or another as the authority for violating this or that or every settled social and political arrangement they encountered. Capital-"s" science is not often heard from these days, but one may still occasionally hear reference to what "science knows" or "science tells us." Apart from being instances of what our English teachers call pathetic fallacies, these references nearly always occur in the context of someone's attempt to sell us something. What they tell the witting is that the author hasn't any idea in the world what "science" is, and hopes that we don't.

Authorities may disagree. Whether disagreement is motivated by real differences or by competition for customers

robert mchenry

Any folly could carry the day in a war of
words: to win, it was only necessary to be
believed.
                    –Barry Unsworth

is beside the point for us onlookers, though we will have to
make our choice eventually on some basis or abandon our
hope of knowing.

God exists, by two falls to a submission.
                    –Monty Python

6: a need to know

> But *everybody*...has one.
>   ...goes there.
>   ...does it.
>   –any teenager

(Even if it were true, which it never is, what conclusion follows? For the teenager it is self-evident that what everybody else has/goes/does, one at very least may and more usually must. But this is not a conclusion arrived at by reason, as any parent of a teenager can tell you but not the teenager in question.)

In the preceding three chapters we have been considering aspects of what we might think of as the technology of knowing – the sensory apparatus, the construction of a knowable world (by means of schemata ranging from neural organization to political ideologies), and the use (whether before, during, or after the decision to know) of evidence. I want to lay these aside now and look behind them, as it were, to the motivation for knowing. Why do we want to know, anyway? Why do we expend the energy, the time that it takes to know things? What's in it for us?

When my sons were young they succumbed to epidemic enthusiasm at a time when sports-oriented trading cards were extremely popular. They bought them with (immediately discarded) bubble gum; they bought them in packs that might, but usually didn't, contain a special, rare, premium card; they bought them from a rather unsavory dealer (subsequently the object of some sort of official inquiry) in a dingy little store near home. They didn't seem much interested in the information printed on the cards, though. Mostly they arranged them in piles or packets or albums, and they spent a ridiculous amount of time consulting an "official" guide to card prices. From time to time one of them would run up with the announcement that *this card right here* was worth ten dollars! or twenty! or a hundred and thirty-five! I would ask "How do you know that?" And the answer, invariably, was, "It says so in this price list." And I would ask, "Would Mr. Unsavory give you that much for the card?" To which the answer was always, "Well, no, of course not." "Would one of your friends give you that much?" "No." "Do you know any way you could actually get that much money for that card?" "No." "Then it isn't worth that much." "Yes, it is. It says so right here." They were quite clear, and quite firm, on the point.

No amount of explanation on my part would convince them otherwise. In part it was youth; they were too young to grasp the fundamental fact of economics, that the value of a good is set by the market, the real market where things are really bought and sold. This is understandable, as a good many people of legally adult years fail to grasp that as well. But it was more: What they *knew* was something they very much *wanted* to know. What I was suggesting as an alternative, however well grounded in economic theory or even just experience, was a great deal less attractive.

Aristotle began his *Metaphysics* with the ringing declaration that "All men by nature desire to know." That sentiment has been a hope or a point of faith for many. But Aristotle didn't say *what* man desires to know, and from his lofty vantage he would hardly recognize as human the desire to know the point spread, how to spoof a firewall, or where Elvis is currently living. Mike Royko, taking full advantage of the lessons available to him from an additional 2,200 years of history and a training stint at the Chicago City News Bureau, in effect replied to Aristotle in asking "If there is so deep a craving for significant information, why do millions watch Roseanne or Beavis and Butt-head?" A more psychologically grounded view of man might revise Aristotle to explain that "All men by nature require to feel that they know." The feeling of knowing, the subjective comfort that comes with unquestioned acceptance of some proposition, any proposition, may be more like what all men desire. And we have seen that this feeling can arise alike from actual knowing and from the state of believing that is so secure that it is indistinguishable from knowing. I know; but, unbeknownst to me, I am wrong. In reality, I only believe; but I don't know it. So I feel OK.

It appears that there is more than one possible motive in the search for knowing. Sometimes my motive is more or less pure curiosity. If I ask "What is the atomic weight of molybdenum?" the chances are that I have not staked anything on the answer, and consequently I can take in just about any answer with equanimity. ("It's 95.94? Good." "37? OK, fine." "673? Whatever.") But sometimes there is something other behind my question than curiosity. If I ask "Where is Elvis living now?" or "What is the real story behind the so-called moon landing?" I have given you, in the form and tone of my questions, reason to suspect that some possible answers would provide me with more pleasure than others, irrespective of whatever happens to be true. I am biased, predisposed toward certain kinds of answer, more likely to accept them than others. (Nor is it necessary that I tip my hand, as in these examples.)

To ask what lies behind the technology is to ask what circumstances had the effect of preserving the elements of the technology as they evolved. Note that this is not the same as asking what caused them to evolve. To speak of a "cause" is to risk serious misunderstanding. Such causes as biologists would acknowledge include the propensity of DNA molecules, which control the development of each new individual organism (by mechanisms largely unknown) to undergo very localized changes from time to time (for reasons not certainly known) and the winnowing process that results from the fact that some of these changes render the particular individual more or less fit for the environment it inhabits. They would not acknowledge the sense of "cause" that could give rise to such a statement as "This characteristic evolved in order to...". There is no direction to evolution, no end point toward which it tends, no final cause, as Aristotle would have called it. At any given moment in evolutionary time, random changes are conserved or abandoned only as they render the individual more or less likely to survive and reproduce in its actual situation.

What does an organism require in order to be fit to survive and reproduce? Generally speaking, it requires energy to complete its physical development and to produce the next generation (either directly, as by fission or budding, or as a contribution to sexual reproduction); in the case of sexually reproducing species, it also needs some degree of access to an appropriately other individual of the species. The energy requirement is typically fulfilled by what we usually call food. Food, as most of us realize, does not simply come when one is hungry. For most animals it must be found, which requires the expenditure of energy. This use of energy in order to acquire more energy gives rise to an internal energy economy in which the expenditure must be met by the energy value of the food found, with a little left over for that other business. Accomplishing this requires some means of finding. For not everything is food. Some things are not food. Indeed, some things turn out to be other creatures who would have us for food. Clearly, it would be advantageous to have some means of detecting possible food and of distinguishing it from non-food and especially from possible eaters-of-us; some means more efficient, with a better win-lose ratio, than just bumping into things, biting into them, and hoping for the best. Enter the senses.

They don't enter just like that, of course. The fact that it would be useful to have something like a sense simply means that should such a thing happen to occur it will have a fair chance of being passed along to offspring. Fitness, not purpose; and likelihood, not certainty.

On the evidence, given time enough, such things do happen, sometimes more than once, as was the case with something really useful like vision. Vision permits an organism to be aware of things that are at some distance from itself, beyond touch and often beyond smell or hearing, and if the organism learns to use it well – meaning, if the development of visual capacity is matched by the development of appropriate neural processing techniques – it can learn to sort those things into meaningful categories, such as food, enemies, mating candidates, shelter, background, and so on. This is a powerful tool for survival.

It is also associated from its inception with powerful feelings : hunger, fear, and the sexual drive. These internal impulses, however differently organized and manifested from species to species, are what motivate much of animal behavior. This is true even of humans, though most of us don't spend our days literally hunting for food, dodging predators, seeking shelter, or attempting to mate (there are notorious exceptions, of course). In human life these drives have come to be mediated by culture and the mechanisms of civilization, so that, for example, hunting has become working for a living, whose connection with food is a chain of abstract economic links. What is to be noted here is the means of motivation. The need for food is not simply a natural circumstance, like the wetness of water or the darkness of night, nor is it conveyed by means of a rule or advisory motto ("Eat from time to time"). The need for food is expressed in the actual living organism as hunger, a feeling that is not pleasant and that thus serves to motivate the organism to undertake certain appropriate behavior. This behavior is aided by information about the world yielded by the senses. The more useful information gathered and processed, the more quickly will productive behavior result, leading not only to the amelioration of the unpleasant feelings but often to the experience of positively pleasant ones. I feel hunger; I look for food; I spot food; I eat food; I feel better.

This early and close association of the tools and methods of knowing with pleasure and the satisfaction of desire is very suggestive. To me it suggests, if not an explanation, at least a context within which our "desire to know" may be placed. It suggests a connection by which the means of achieving the satisfaction of some very specific needs might in the course of time become a source of a more generalized kind of satisfaction, of pleasure in and of itself. From being able to know where the food is (and hence how to achieve a specific sort of satisfaction) we develop a knack of just knowing where stuff is, food or not, and find that we take a generalized sort of pleasure in the act of knowing. We find, too, that the obverse has come to be the case: Not knowing becomes, in itself, a source of discontent. And a discontent, as a species of discomfort, can be a motive.

> The natural man dislikes the dis-ease which
> accompanies the doubtful and is ready to
> take almost any means to end it. Uncertainty
> is got rid of by fair means or foul.
> —John Dewey

So it is that we find ourselves seeking knowledge not only for particular purposes, which become ever more numerous and diverse as civilization evolves, but also for no particular purpose, just to, as we say, satisfy our "curiosity."

(Knowing as a cure for the distress of not-knowing is the key to those popular television game shows that are simply formalized trivia contests. The really successful contestants, those who enlist the sympathies of the audience and thus best serve the business aspect of the show, are not those who know the answers cold and don't hesitate to snap them out. Those contestants often strike us as vaguely unsympathetic, perhaps a little arrogant, in short as know-it-alls, whom nobody much cares for. No, the popular ones are those who allow us to share in the drama of knowing.

> "Alright, Anita, here's your question: 'When was the War of Jenkins' Ear?'"
>
> "Oh, um... just a minute...I know this...[the tension begins]...I think I know this...[we observe and empathize with the anxiety of her uncertainty]....Was it...1739?" [We hold our collective breath.]
>
> "Yes! That's absolutely correct!" [release, relief, and — for Anita — reward]

Whew!)

More seriously, the need to know may sometimes drive us to improbable, even desperate methods, such as consulting oracles (also known, in different times and places, as soothsayers, haruspices, diviners, fortune tellers, visionaries, and consultants).

> Being a visionary is a new profession, but it is really just a variant on fortunetelling, which may be the world's oldest. And its marketing appeal is similar – people will pay for reassurance about the unknown. The fortunetellers of old had many techniques. Yet the crystal balls and tea leaves are just apparatus. All fortunetelling, in fact, rests on three pillars.

First, you must tell people more or less what
you think they want to hear. Second, you
must spice your predictions with drama.
Nobody wants a prediction that the future
will be more or less like the present, even if
that is, statistically speaking, an excellent
prediction....

Third, your predictions must somehow avoid
measurements of their accuracy. Many tricks
have been invented to serve this end.
Predictions can be vague, for example, or
couched in complicated gibberish. Either
way, there is a loophole. And customers
generally don't mind: Seeking advice about
the future is more about relieving insecurity
or anxiety than about achieving statistical
accuracy.
　　　　　　　　　—Nathan Myhrvold

If this is at least plausible as a sketch of a model, and it is
certainly nothing more than that, then we can justify Aristotle's
claim about us and also begin to understand how Royko's
complaint comes about. Not knowing – which, as we have
established, must mean the feeling of not knowing, the
awareness of not knowing, as distinct from really not knowing
– produces a type of discomfort. In order to eliminate that
discomfort, we set about to know whatever it is we are
conscious of not knowing. Because the number of things that
any one of us might not know is effectively infinite, this
becomes a permanent condition of our lives. There's always
something, it seems, that we don't know, and so we're always
stalking this bit of knowledge or that one. Eventually we find it,
and experience a moment of pleasure (which, we discover, we
can relive in various ways, such as by exhibiting our bits of
knowledge at cocktail parties); or, on the other hand, we don't

find it and are irritated enough either to try harder or to give it up (which we can do because our actual survival is not at stake).

Notice what well known and (at least superficially) popular concept does not play a role in this story as we have told it so far: truth.

"Whoa!" I hear you say. "How can this be? Truth not a part of the story? Surely you jest."

I said that it doesn't play a role *so far*. Of course it may come in, but not where we might have assumed. It doesn't come in at the motivation stage, at least not necessarily. If it comes in at all, it is usually later. Seeing how it comes in requires us to think for a moment – only that – about what we mean by "truth." In fact, we mean a great many things by it, and trying to pin them down and sort them out has been one of the chief occupations of philosophers. For our purposes we can focus on one simple kind of meaning, the one in which a statement is said to be true if it in some demonstrable way represents, or as it is sometimes phrased "corresponds to," how things actually are. Now, this apparently innocuous formulation is in fact rife with problems, but it will do for us. If I say "I know that it is Tuesday," and it is in fact Tuesday, then what I say I know corresponds to the actual state of the world. Therefore it is true and I am entitled to claim to know it. I say to you "It is Tuesday," and if you are the sensible person I think you are, you check it out. This may involve nothing more than comparing what I claim to what you already know; or it may involve doing a little research, such as looking at the masthead of today's newspaper. "Yes," you conclude, "you're right; it is Tuesday." This is as much as to say "What you say is true."

As noted, there are problems with this naive idea of "true." For example, it is not always clear, under this definition, what to make of a statement like "The War of Jenkins' Ear took place in 1739." What things in the real world can we point to, to which this statement or the various terms in it correspond? It's all in the past, which no longer exists in the ordinary sense of the verb. (Perhaps you will argue that the statement corresponds to certain other statements to be found in documents, history books, and the like. I will then suggest that, on that view, a Xerox® machine is an unerring fount of Truth.) Or what to do with "The present king of France is bald" (there being no such person); or with "I find your obstinacy mildly irritating" (you having no way to observe my mood in order to determine that it is in fact one of irritation)?

Notwithstanding, for the kinds of statements we have mostly been using to illustrate our points, this simple idea of truth will suffice. In this practical view of the meaning of "true," it turns out to be a way of testing what we "know" against something else. The something else might be the world itself (as when I claim that it is raining, and you look out the window to see for yourself), or it might be social convention (as with the Tuesday business), or it might be with standing claims to truth that we agree to accept, perhaps because they have already been tested (as when I claim Elvis was born in Memphis, and you look it up in the encyclopedia and correct me on the basis of what you read there). The testing is never perfect and never assures us beyond any doubt. You may mistake the effects of a lawn sprinkler for rain; the newspaper may be yesterday's; the encyclopedia may be marred by typographical or other sorts of errors.

Some claims may never be tested, or they may not be tested effectively. I may choose, for reasons hard to imagine, to claim to have been born in Peculiar, Missouri (yes, there is such a place). So long as I take care not to make the claim in front of the three or four living persons who actually know better, I am pretty certain not to be challenged. Of course, there is documentary evidence to the contrary, but it would require some exertion to find and bring it forth, and unless there were something substantial at stake, who would bother? And I can go on asserting that the War of Jenkins' Ear took place in 1683, or whatever, as long as no one cares to look into the matter, and you probably have a fairly shrewd idea of how likely that is. This is true *whether or not I myself know it's wrong.*

Let's consider that for a moment. We have already established that my sense of knowing, the subjective certainty I have in some proposition, is independent of whether it is true or not. I am capable of "knowing" any quantity of things that are not the case. Why would I permit such a state of affairs to persist? Why would I not test what I believe I know? To begin with, I don't just *believe* I know it – I know it. I have no obvious motive to test it. If I know it, it has already met some criterion. It's just that the criterion wasn't truth. In fact, I'm apt to consider it true because I know it, even though logically it ought to work the other way round.

At a minimum, it met the criterion of being something for me to know. If I have, as we have imagined, a kind of generalized need to know, or rather a need not to not-know, then almost any sort of knowledgey-looking item might be acceptable. What day is it? If there are no other requirements than that I have some answer, then any of the seven possibilities will do. If there is to be additional testing, of course, then the field will be narrowed. If there is to be additional testing, I will take more care in deciding what I know. But if not, I may be quite satisfied with a random selection or one governed by some other consideration (I've always been particularly partial to Thursday; so let it be Thursday). Some void has been filled, however badly and insecurely.

Attending so crudely, so carelessly, to the raw need to not not-know can become pathological. The know-it-all, the person who is never at a loss for an answer (not necessarily *the* answer, just an) and who is never wrong (in his own estimation, at least), is a social blight, a well-known drag, and sometimes a little scary.

> I always know.
> —Jim Thompson

A variant of the type is the person who, though less obtrusively knowing than the last, is satisfied he needn't learn anything more, especially from you.

> Think of your brain as a large jar which is already quite full. So don't put any more in it because it might spill all over, which is not a pretty sight, and anyway you know most everything you need to.
> —Nicole Hollander

A second very popular motive for knowing was suggested by the sports-card anecdote. It is often the case that, given a choice from among several alternative things to know, we will choose one that is attractive, that will give us pleasure, that will be comforting.

> They didn't want to be taught, having already decided what they preferred to believe.
> —P.D. James

As long as we can avoid, or deny, evidence to the contrary, we cling to this kind of knowledge as to a security blanket. Here is a little self-test: How are you as a judge of character? That is, How accurate are your judgments about other people, especially when you first meet? Do you size them up pretty shrewdly? Can you tell the good ones from the rest? Are you of average ability in this, below average, or above average? Here's another: How good a driver are you? Average? Below or above average?

Welcome to "Lake Wobegon," where all the children, miraculously, are above average. Most people, it seems, are better-than-average judges of character, and most people are better-than-average drivers, too. Just ask them. How can this be? Actually, it's mathematically possible, but it would require a very peculiar and highly unlikely distribution of these faculties across the population. A more plausible explanation is that there are some things we simply wish to believe, perhaps need to believe, about ourselves. They give us pleasure or comfort, and they are part of how we prefer, or need, to see ourselves. It is a small and common foible, clinging to such beliefs, but it can skew our judgments about real matters and affect our behavior in real situations.

Then there is the knowledge we take on authority. As we saw in the last chapter, it is necessary to resort to authority if our knowledge of the world is to extend beyond the small sphere of our own direct experience. What can pose problems is the way we choose which authorities to embrace (we use an interesting metaphor for this relationship, don't we?) and the fervor of that embrace.

There are perfectly good grounds for relying on authorities, of course. They are, after all – some of them, anyway – *authorities*. This is to say, there is a class of things called "authorities." Some of the members of the class are in it because that is precisely what they are, and in fact the class takes its name from them. They are experts, they are acknowledged as reliable sources, they may be appealed to and cited with confidence: they really, really *know* (as well as does anyone). Then there are the members who have got in by other means.

The sad fact is that there are no entry requirements, no qualifying exams, no standards of performance, no dues, nothing to separate the sheep from the goats, the wheat from the chaff, except one thing: To be a member of the class of authorities, somebody has to agree that you are one. Somebody; anybody. In truth, that's the whole game. You are an authority if you say so and somebody else, anybody else, chooses to treat you as one. (This is the explanation for Mr. Blackwell.) The chief reason you would want to be one is precisely to be so treated. It's nice being an authority (or so I hear). You get listened to; you get mentioned; you might get a couple of bucks; you might even find yourself in position to wield influence, power, the other kind of authority. Here we see revealed at last the transaction model of authority we stumbled upon in the last chapter. I treat you as an authority: You pronounce something to be true, a piece of knowledge, and I (figuratively) buy it, meaning I accept it as knowledge on your authority. In this transaction, I get something to know, with little effort, and the comfort of a "good" reason to know it, and you get to be an authority because I accept what you say and acknowledge that you are, indeed, my authority. *Quid pro quo* and QED.

"It shouldn't be that easy!" you protest, and I can only agree. It's easy and getting easier, it seems.

> We're perpetually warned about the contemporary rise of cynicism, but a parallel American contagion, often infecting the same citizens, is credulity. The postmodern cynic cum naïf mistrusts the government, the media, and the other élites even as he recklessly embraces this or that line of grassroots make-believe. You believe that a

majority of women were sexually abused as
children? You believe that Ben Franklin was
an anti-Semitic propagandist? You believe
that you have seen a documentary videotape
of government doctors performing an
autopsy on a captured extraterrestrial?
Whatever.

> –Kurt Andersen

We pays our money (merely figuratively sometimes,
sometimes not) and we takes our choice. This authority or that
one? The one I choose, of course, will be the real, the true
authority. The one I reject will be, depending on the nature of
the case and on my mental state and my emotional needs,
something between simply less authoritative and an outright
fraud, or co-conspirator. If this seems a bit cynical, then try
Friedrich Nietzsche:

> What makes one regard philosophers half
> mistrustfully and half mockingly is not that
> one again and again detects how innocent
> they are – how often and how easily they fall
> into error and go astray, in short their
> childishness and childlikeness – but that they
> display altogether insufficient honesty, while
> making a mighty and virtuous noise as soon
> as the problem of truthfulness is even
> remotely touched on. They pose as having
> discovered and attained their real opinions
> through the self-evolution of a cold, pure,
> divinely unperturbed dialectic...: while what
> happens at bottom is that a prejudice, a
> notion, an "inspiration," generally a desire of
> the heart sifted and made abstract, is
> defended by them with reasons sought after
> the event....

The question remains, then: How do we choose our authorities? Because they ask or demand to be chosen? Because they offer a quick way to ease the pain of not knowing? Because they have a record of being right? Because lots of other people have chosen them? Because they claim to know more, and more certainly, than the others? Because they remind us of someone else? Because they flatter us by even asking for our attention and then our allegiance? (Hint: There's one good reason hidden in there.)

So how many different motives for "I know" have we covered? Let's see; I know x because

> ...it's easy.
> ...it's comforting.
> ...I picked it.
> ...you don't.
> ...everybody knows it.
> ...certain people know it.
> ...I'm the kind of person who knows it.
> ...I wish to be seen as the kind of person who knows it.

Anything else? Oh, yeah --

> ...I've tested it and it seems to be true.

It is of crucial importance to bear in mind the responsibility we assume when we claim to know something. We are telling others and (if we are sincere) ourselves that such-and-such is the case, is true of the world, and that therefore they (or we) may confidently act on that basis. In effect, we are saying to the blind pedestrian, "Go ahead; the light is green." It is also prudent to remember that the process of evolution that got us here is a house game, one that the players lose more often than they win. We are a bet that a species that is driven by two conflicting needs – to poke its nose into everything, take it apart, and see what makes it go, and on the other hand to find the quickest, easiest, but not necessarily best way to satisfy that need – can live long and prosper. Sucker bet? It's up to you.

7: prudence and the 3 c's

Maybe yes, maybe no, maybe maybe. –Bob
Clampett (or perhaps Stan Freberg)

Let's sum up. In Chapter 2 we decided that, while we have
some rough idea of when to say "I know" or, alternatively, "I
believe," we don't really have any way of telling if we get it
right. No green light goes on in our heads when what we think
we know happens to be true, and no red one in the opposite
case. Knowing the truth and "knowing" falsity can feel exactly
the same. In Chapter 3 we decided that the information on
which we base our knowing comes to us through the senses
and that, while there is good reason to trust the evidence of
the senses much of the time, they are subject to error or
distortion. In any case, there is no reason to assume that they
give us a complete picture of how the world "really" is,
whatever that might mean. In Chapter 4 we decided that
sense data alone do not a world make; it takes an organizing
scheme, or rather countless such schemes, operating at many,
many levels, to bring some useful order out of, and thus find
human meaning in, the reports of the senses. No scheme, no
sense. In Chapter 5 we decided that when we at last conclude
that we know something, we have built our sense of knowing
on one of two possible foundations: evidence gotten on our
own, or some sort of authority, which must find its way back to
evidence somewhere or be quite without foundation. In
Chapter 6 we considered the various motives for knowing and
began to sense the various traps they create for the unwary.

With this all in mind, let's now revisit our cautionary tales from
Chapter 1 and diagnose each case of knowing what wasn't so.

The Salinger case, the most recent and technology-rich of the four, is also, for our purposes, the simplest. Pierre Salinger, it seems apparent, needed to know. That is, he needed to feel that he was in possession of real, and not merely real but inside, information – the *really* real stuff, in other words. He was, after all, long accustomed to knowing what was really going on in and behind great affairs. He was also accustomed to believing in certain kinds of evidence, the kinds that come from behind the public surface of things. And finally, he was evidently unaware of how open the Internet had become to users of all sorts, including paranoid fantasists. (If someone had shown him the Nazi moonbase site, or any of a thousand similar examples of the free expression of nonsense, perhaps this incident would never have occurred.) In short, the need to know outweighed whatever care or doubt he might have applied before deciding that he did, in fact, know. And once he *knew*, he had no way to detect that he didn't really know. And so he made a bit of a fool of himself.

If you found nothing peculiar about the document Salinger believed, you might consider returning to Chapter 4, though it may not do you any good. If, on the other hand, you are wondering how anyone could possibly have taken it seriously, you are perhaps too quick to judge. The alleged report of an unnamed someone, offered unvouched-for by an anonymous writer via a medium that provides no mechanism for validation, is perhaps this age's equivalent to the slicker's offer to sell the Brooklyn Bridge to the newly arrived rube. The difference may be that now, in the Information Age, anybody can play the slicker and everybody is apt be a rube.

It was a perfectly ordinary mistake, of a kind we all make. We find ourselves in a situation where preserving pride, face, reputation, or advantage requires that we step beyond what we actually know and to claim to know what we don't really know. The difference is that when we are shown to be wrong we usually suffer briefly and more or less privately, whereas

Salinger, as a public figure, was held up to ridicule in the press. Let us be thankful, you and I, for our obscurity.

The case of General DeWitt is also one of needing to know but with a couple of crucial differences. First, DeWitt was under heavy and growing pressure, from the public, from politicians, from his superiors, and from the examples of the unlucky commanders at Pearl Harbor, to "know" a certain thing, namely that the ethnic Japanese of California constituted a real and present danger. Second, the consequence of his "knowing" this particular thing was enormous; something like 120,000 persons, most of them American citizens and all of them innocent of any crime, were forced to sell or abandon homes, farms, businesses, and possessions and to live for months or years in internment camps.

Look again at the climactic sentence in his report:

> "The very fact that no sabotage has taken place to date is a disturbing and confirming indication that such action will be taken."

It may help in seeing the underlying structure of the argument to apply it in different contexts. Thus:

The very fact that North Dakota has not yet declared war on France is disturbing and confirming indication that it will do so.

The very fact that the Moon has not yet turned rancid is disturbing and confirming indication that it will.

The very fact that Paris Hilton has not yet been elected President is disturbing and confirming indication that she will be.

The argument says, in more general words, "I confess I can find no ground for a claim to know *x*; nonetheless, for various reasons unconnected with the facts of the matter, I claim to know *x*." What made this illogic admissible in the creation of official policy was the volatile chemical reaction of rhetoric with fear and greed. A great many people found it necessary or convenient or both to know this particular *x*.

The Lysenko episode is very complex. It is not at all obvious who knew what, or whether any knowing – as distinct from believing, accepting, or acting-as-though – was present at all. Lysenko himself was clearly clever and an opportunist; but how cynical he might have been – that is, whether he really believed all or any of what he preached – is beyond our knowing. Likewise his supporters; did they believe, or were they simply grabbing at the main chance? And Stalin; did he "know" that genetics is merely bourgeois pseudoscience? Did he care?

Whatever the mix of knowing and acting-as-though may have been, the net product was a system of propositions about biology that was represented as knowledge and that was taught as such in the schools and universities. If you lived in the Soviet Union or one of its satellite nations in those days and studied biology, you were supposed to know in the Lysenko way. If you failed to know thus, or at least to behave as though you did, you were liable to severe consequences.

What ultimately doomed Lysenkoism (apart from the always unpredictable turns of political power and allegiances in the Soviet Union) was its utter lack of foundation in the real world. It was a system constructed to conform to an elaborate big-I

Ideology, Marxism, that was held to be the source of all truth. True philosophy, true science, true social organization, all were deemed to flow ineluctably from the Marxist analysis of the nature of the world. Persons rose or fell in favor, survived or perished, according to how closely they adhered to orthodox Marxism and how publicly they demonstrated their adherence. (One of the very senior positions in the government was the official ideologist, who dictated what was and what was not in conformity with orthodox Marxism.) It was not permitted to wonder how likely it was that one man, even one as brilliant as Karl Marx, could sit in a library, even one as grand as the British Museum, and simply think out and write down an explanation for the whole of human life on Earth. But Marx had done so, and for reasons and by means that lie far beyond the scope of this book (and beyond me, too) his views had been taken up and turned into absolute dogma by some very ruthless and in time very powerful political leaders. After that, the rest followed: all public knowledge, belief, discussion, and action had to conform.

A simplistic explanation of all things, a paranoid political system, a few executions, the usual quota of opportunists – by now we know the story pretty well. And we're pretty sure it couldn't happen here, to us, right?

There is plenty of precedent in human history for this kind of enforced knowing. Any number of theologies and philosophies have provided answers to such great questions as What is the nature of Man? or of Life? or of the Universe? or of God? and have devised tools for creating conforming answers to all subsidiary questions. Proper use of these tools tells us how various aspects of the world ought to be, given the original grand vision. So long as we care only about ought-to-be, we can choose whichever grand vision best suits us and memorize the details. It is when we come to ask what actually is, or (since the true believer isn't supposed to ask that) when, having closed our eyes, we bump our noses against what is, that the problems begin.

So we come to the last of our tales, which was the first. The easiest view to take about Croesus is that he, too, heard what he wanted to hear and thus "knew" what he needed to know. And that's true. But by this time we've come to expect that in these tales (and perhaps we are beginning to suspect it in ourselves, too). For me the interesting part of the story happens earlier, when Croesus in effect auditions the various oracles before deciding which one to consult on the great question of war. All of the oracles claim to be authoritative. The essence of an oracle, after all, is to be in direct communication with a god and to have thereby access to truth. But unlike Pierre Salinger, Croesus suspects that some oracles might be like some Web sites, loud and opinionated but unreliable. He devises a test, or in other words he conducts an experiment, to see which oracle actually performs as advertised. Delphi wins. His mistake comes afterward, when Delphi gives him that artfully ambiguous answer.

It is not known with certainty what happened then to Croesus. He may have become a member of Cyrus' court and perhaps a provincial governor. Herodotus tells of his despair after the fall of Sardis and of his reproaching the god who, he believed, had falsely encouraged him to go to war. The oracle replied that he had no right

> to complain with respect to the oracular
> answer which he received. For when the god
> told him that, if he attacked the Persians, he
> would destroy a mighty empire, he ought, if
> he had been wise, to have sent again and
> inquired which empire was meant, that of
> Cyrus or his own; but if he neither
> understood what was said, nor took the

trouble to seek for enlightenment, he has
only himself to blame for the result.

Hard words. Tough god.

The question posed by these bad examples and by this whole
book, then, is How can I do better? To this purely practical
question there ought to be practical answers, as indeed there
are. But the very first step toward a practical approach to
knowing is to recognize that behind this question of How? lurks
another that must be faced and answered before the work of
knowing begins, and it is this: Am I sure I want to?

Am I sure that I want to know *x* and thereby risk having to
give up believing *y*? Am I willing to discover that I might have
to give up the comfort of *y* without even getting an assured *x*
in return? In other words, what if what is actually the case (so
far as I am honestly able to find it out) is less attractive, less
satisfying than some alternative, quite possibly the alternative
I have been contentedly "knowing" up to now? What if knowing
what is really so will oblige me to discard my accustomed
beliefs? What if it will oblige me to act against the conventions
or prejudices of my peers, or against my own immediate
material interest? What is it really worth to me to know
something, in light of the fact that I could – perhaps with less
effort, stress, and cost – "know" something else? These are
hard questions. They do not arise at full strength in every
knowing situation, of course; they do not arise (for me,
anyway) in the matter of the atomic weight of molybdenum.
But when they do arise they are very hard.

Most of us are not heroes, prepared to sacrifice all (or even a
lot) in the cause of truth. Most of us, in fact, often settle well
short.

how to know

> Doth any man doubt, that if there were
> taken out of men's minds vain opinions,
> flattering hopes, false valuations,
> imaginations as one would, and the like, but
> it would leave the minds of a number of men
> poor shrunken things, full of melancholy and
> indisposition, and unpleasing to themselves?
> —Francis Bacon

If you are prepared to decide that at least sometimes you will risk knowing, we can press on.

A couple of hints have been dropped already. I gave Croesus a grudging nod on the ground that he took the trouble to evaluate the competing claims of various oracles. We've talked about looking up facts, seeking corroboration for what we think we know, in short, checking things out.

> If your mother says she loves you, check it
> out.
> —Arnold Dornfeld

There's nothing of rocket science in the idea of checking things out (though some applications of the principle, such as checking out the composition of rocks on Mars, may require rocket science in the execution). It's more a matter of the selection of things to be checked and the care with which the checking is done.

A good beginning in the selection process is to look to the ideas we already have about the matter at hand. Our sense of the nature and significance of the matter, of what the relevant facts are, and even of what are to count as facts in this realm – all of this has been shaped by previously formed ideas that we have accepted and used as lenses through which to view our world and that up to this moment we may not have examined or questioned. Clearly, if our goal is to find out as nearly as we can how things are, we want to be viewing them through the clearest, plainest, least distorting lenses we can find.

More generally, we need to work from a basis of fewer rather than more assumptions about what ought to be, fewer rather than more prejudgments about what the processes of examination will reveal. Fewer, but not none, as we understood in Chapter 4, for intelligibility itself depends on the structure provided by some basic organizing schemes and concepts, beginning with the idea that there is a real world out there capable of containing the matters of our concern, and working up from there. As we have also come to understand, identifying our assumptions, prejudgments, habitual ways of seeing, automatic responses, and the like can be most difficult. The history of art offers instructive examples. It is conventional wisdom that the discovery of the principles of visual perspective and their incorporation into art was one of the earliest and most important achievements of what we now call the Renaissance. Before this development, artists working in two dimensions, painters, used a variety of conventionalized techniques to indicate the spatial relationships in their pictures or, sometimes, to signal that there were none. When we look at these pictures we find it hard to read them; without often being able to pinpoint what is "wrong" with them, we feel that the geometry doesn't work. Sometimes they appear to consist of bits of different pictures pasted together. During the first half of the 15th century a new way of drawing that had begun to emerge was carefully analyzed. It was a way of depicting on the flat surface of a painting the geometrical relationships that obtain among solid objects in space. Books of technique were published so that all artists could attempt to master the new method, called the method of perspective. Mastery involved learning to identify vanishing points, to lay out or imagine a gridwork of trapezoids on the surface and identifying it with another gridwork, real or imagined, of rectangles in front of the scene to be drawn. Over the course of a century, the new method achieved virtually universal adoption, but it was not an easy victory.

The discovery of perspective is now understood to have been an essential part of a profound change in the way we view the world, a change that has directly produced our modern scientific-technological culture. But notice the oddity in this: To draw in perspective is to draw *as we actually see*, in terms of the physics of vision. Learning to draw in this way was in fact a matter of unlearning to draw in some other way. That other way was, in essence, drawing as the artist understood things actually to be, according to some preexisting notion of what is really real. The unreflective act of seeing blends the optics and biology that produce sensory data with whatever interpretational schemes we use unconsciously to impute meaning to the patterns we detect. Change the schemes and the meaning changes accordingly. But our seeing is so habituated, so constant, that it requires great effort and discipline to see through, as it were, the schemes to the perceptions themselves.

In the 19th century the painter Claude Monet experimented with painting what he was really seeing rather than what, ordinarily, he would have assumed he was seeing. In various series, as of haystacks or a cathedral, he sought to capture the effects of changing light through the course of a day or through the procession of seasons. To do so he had to avoid painting the stone of the cathedral as he "knew" it to look and to focus consciously on how it actually appeared to him at a particular moment. As he wrote to a friend:

> I am hard at it; I am bent upon a series of
> different effects but at this time of year the
> sun declines so quickly that I cannot follow
> it....[T]he further I go, the more I see that

123

one has to work a lot in order to express
what I am looking for: "instantaneity," above
all the atmosphere, the same light diffused
everywhere.... In short, I am more and more
determined to render what I experience.

We are not usually called upon to dig so deeply into our
structure of interpretational schemes and to make such
profound changes. What is indispensable is that we be aware
of what lies between the data and the knowledge.

The proposition that lies before us, inviting our assent, must
be tried, tested in various ways against what we already (think
we) know, whatever of that is left after we have evaluated our
assumptions. One key test is that of consistency. Is this
candidate proposition consistent with what we have already
decided is the case? Consistency matters because – this is a
piece of Chapter 4 little-i ideology – we can't construct any
kind of world without it. It is a strong and indispensable
constraint on how we assemble bits and pieces, facts and
patterns, into an intelligible world. Experience and reason
agree that it is a natural consequence of there being a real,
working world out there whose workings are regular and have
both produced and shaped us and our consciousness.

You can perfectly well believe contradictory
things, for example that you can cheat on
your diet and still lose weight. But you
cannot *know* contradictory things, because
knowledge must be consistent.
                    –Richard Watson

If the candidate proposition is consistent with our prior
knowledge, does that make it true? That would be too easy. In
fact, all we can infer is that the candidate has escaped being

discarded because of inconsistency. A false proposition could conceivably pass the consistency test. Still more unfortunately, an inconsistent candidate isn't necessarily false. There is always the possibility, though perhaps a very small one, that the candidate is true and points to a long overlooked weakness in our prior knowledge. Disconcerting though this possibility may be – and it is that, because it seems to leave us with no way of certainly determining the truth or falsity of a candidate piece of new knowledge – it is of enormous importance. Without this possibility, error once committed and accepted into our body of knowledge could never be corrected. The edifice of human knowledge would grow and grow, incorporating unknown and uncounted errors, never to be detected and eliminated, with the result that the whole structure would become more and more unstable, incompetent, and liable to crash. It would, that is, be indistinguishable from a mere Ideology.

The next test is comparison with experience. The experience may be our own; or it may be that of others, suitably organized, recorded, and attested – in other words, it may be authority. In either case, as we have seen, it carries some degree of uncertainty. Our own experience is grounded finally in sense data, which are incomplete, subject to various sorts of distortion, and in any case are in themselves unintelligible. Authority we have learned to treat with caution. In either case, we are again looking for consistency, and for the same reason. And again, finding consistency guarantees nothing, and neither does finding inconsistency.[1]

A further test is comparison with consequences. If x is true, I may reason, then it should also be the case that y. I look to see if y is true, or plausible, or possible. If it is not, I must conclude that there is a deep problem with x. This was how Croesus dealt with the claims of the competing oracles. In that case, x = the claim to be able to answer questions truthfully and y = the answer to the particular test question posed by the king. In those cases where *y* turned out to be false, he concluded that *x* was also false; when Delphi passed the *y* test, he accepted its *x* claim. (I assume in this that no rules of logic are violated in drawing inferences. Many errors of this sort are possible, and some are common.)

The process I am describing may strike you as simple common sense (than which, as wags have long noted, few things are less common). If you recall the discussion in Chapter 4 you may recognize it as a simple application of the scientific method, so called. I say "so called" because so many intellectual sins have been committed in the name of "science." Such as this:

> "Why, man," he bellowed, "it's medieval
> science all over again! *Step one*, you sneak
> up on a phenomenon. *Step two*, you zap it
> with your patented catchall theory. *Step
> three, Conclusum est!* you announce another
> victory over Nature! Next patient, please,
> and all that. Real successful method; kept
> Europe asleep for a thousand years."
> —Robert Grudin

Or this:

> The McCray Refrigerator has the approval of
> scientific men everywhere.
> —advertisement, 1912

Or this: When my older son was in seventh grade I "helped" him with his science project. (The quotes around "helped" indicate that he might have been better off without me.) We built a simple apparatus with which to duplicate Galileo's experiment with a ball rolling down an incline in order to determine how its speed changes over time. We began with the obvious hypothesis, the prevailing belief since Aristotle, that the ball would accelerate at a constant rate. We ran a hundred trials at various distances, timed the ball, and plotted the results. We found that Aristotle was wrong. We then looked for a pattern, a formula, that would describe what actually happened. As best we could estimate, the acceleration was proportional not to the rolling time but to the square of that time. That was our conclusion, and I was pleased both with the outcome (it was correct) and with what we had both learned in conducting the project. Unfortunately, we didn't do very well competitively. It turns out that in "science" (*i.e.*, what is taught as science in seventh grade), you are supposed to prove your original hypothesis true, so that you can tidily restate it at the end. You are not supposed to disprove it and then raise some entirely new hypothesis. As for the fact that a substantial body of thought in the philosophy of science agrees that you cannot finally and unambiguously prove a positive hypothesis and that science generally progresses by disproving instead – well, you can't argue with the teacher.

Nonetheless, science, properly understood, is the best example and model of careful knowing available. Properly understanding science involves especially understanding that it makes essential use of mathematics and that it carefully limits itself to those domains and aspects of the world that are successfully modeled mathematically. (Why any aspect of the world should be so may or may not constitute a mystery. It seems clear that, without actually explaining anything, it is unlikely that we would have evolved and conserved the ability to reason mathematically if such an ability had found no correspondence in the world.) Science, in other words, is a much elaborated and rigorously applied version of what we would like to think of as commonsense reasoning, with the addition of one very special mental tool. It offers itself to us nonscientists as a model precisely because it has been used, analyzed, criticized, and refined so carefully for a couple of centuries. We may not be able to apply its methods in detail to our everyday issues of knowing, but in outline it is a good guide.

And, in fact, we've already covered a good deal of that outline:

- Step 1, clear away all unnecessary assumptions and unwarranted anticipations (such as the conventional or magical "explanations" that scientists often confront).
- Step 2, compare with what is left, comprising what we're pretty sure about (or the standing body of coherent scientific knowledge).
- Step 3, compare with experience (or what the scientist might prefer to call observational data).
- Step 4, draw out some consequences (or predictions) and test them (conduct experiments).

Suppose that our candidate piece of knowledge has survived all this. If you were a scientist, you might now publish your findings about it, perhaps calling it something like "a plausible hypothesis" that was suggested by observation and supported by experimental testing. Other scientists would be invited to try to duplicate your findings and thereby to confirm them (or not; such famous cases as "anomalous water" and "cold fusion" remind us that scientists can go badly wrong sometimes, which is why the publish-and-review process is of critical importance). After a time, the candidate might become generally accepted. But is it true? Would the scientist who developed it originally say so? He might, of course, being but human, but if he were a careful scientist he would not. He would instead say something like "It is supported by all the evidence so far, after testing by several people, and therefore may become a provisional part of our knowledge." It is provisional because it is possible that some new observation will challenge it or that some alternative hypothesis will prove superior; and it will remain provisional because *that possibility can never be entirely eliminated.*

And if the candidate piece of knowledge fails one of these tests? Are you forbidden to believe it? Not at all. I would claim that you cannot claim to know it, but you are free to believe as you will, provided only that you acknowledge the difference.

No; that's wrong. You are free not only to believe as you will but also to believe what you will about what you believe. If you so choose, you can regard your belief as knowledge. Not I nor anyone else has standing to require otherwise of you (not in most countries, anyway).

It's only this: If you ignore the failure and choose to "know" regardless, you then build what is quite likely an error into your personal structure of knowledge, an error that will not only stand uncorrected but will compound itself over time, allowing and even attracting further error. If that's your way, no one can stop you.

We are not scientists, most of us, and we seldom trouble to publish the results of our private knowledge-seeking (though we may well submit them informally to review, by friends or colleagues). This leaves us vulnerable to a kind of error we noted earlier, the kind induced by the attractiveness of ideas arising in our own heads as compared to those trying to get in from outside. Even ideas that did actually arrive from outside – and, to be honest, this is most of them – may have been adopted, gained our affection, become part of us, to the extent that they enjoy the privilege of position irrespective both of their origin and, most important, of how good or true they may be.

It is difficult to follow the example of the scientist in that last step, labeling our new piece of knowledge as provisional.

Provisional knowledge – what we called in Chapter 2 knowledge on probation, knowledge that we consciously hold out at arm's length because we don't yet quite trust it, because it might yet prove to be not true – makes us uncomfortable, very like the discomfort of not knowing at all. It seems only fair that, having made all that effort, we should be rewarded with real knowledge, not just a sort-of-maybe-if-nothing-goes-wrong kind of knowledge. Comes then, if we are not watchful, our will-to-know (or rather our will-to-not-not-know) to the rescue, converting all our provisional knowledge to certainty. Of course, it does no such thing. It converts our discomfort to comfort by allowing us to forget what we have learned about the uncertain nature of all our knowledge. What we know, and how we feel about what we know, or wish to know, are utterly separate matters, and the mixing of them is the source of enormous mischief.

It comes down, finally, to a weighing of probabilities. We cannot demonstrate that a candidate piece of knowledge is certainly, absolutely, true. We can judge that it is almost certainly true, or that it is probably true, or that it might be true, or that it is probably not true....We can, if we wish, make exceedingly fine comparisons of degrees of likelihood, though we are liable to make mistakes when we try. (Just our lousy luck that knowledge depends on something for which we have so little natural talent.) But there it is. Just as the quantum physicist cannot say which hole the electron passes through, so we can only make our best guess. We do have some control over just how good that guess is, but we can never eliminate altogether the maybe element.

In thinking of the process of knowledge formation as a series of exercises in probability estimation, it pays to remember a basic fact about the mathematics of probability: When an event depends upon the joint occurrence of several prior conditions, its probability is the product of the probabilities of those conditions. That is, if A and B and C have to be true in order for D to be true, then the probability that D is true is calculated by multiplying the individual probabilities of A, B, and C. This is important to remember because of the following implication: Numerically, a dead certainty is conventionally assigned a probability of 1. Anything less probable than absolute certainty has a value between 1 and 0. For example, the likelihood that there is a real world outside my consciousness is, by my estimation, very, very close to 1. The likelihood that the water in my glass will stream up to the ceiling as I write this is very, very close to 0. Midway, along about 0.5, is the likelihood that the next coin I flip will turn up heads. And so on. So when you start multiplying various probabilities together, the best that can happen at any given step is no change (the result of multiplying by 1); anything else will make the product smaller. Nothing in heaven or on earth can make it bigger. To give you an idea of how quickly this can affect a final estimate of probability, suppose we have a series of prior events, each of which has a pretty high probability, 0.9. It takes only six of these chained together to make the resulting joint probability , the probability of something that is contingent on those six prior conditions, just a hair better than a coin toss.

We can imagine the testing of a candidate piece of knowledge as just such a joint probability calculation. It might look like this:

P (the probability that the candidate is true) = P_1 (the probability that I exist; bowing to Descartes, we'll give this one, and only this one, a 1) x P_2 (the probability that there is a real world; let's say this is 0.99999...) x P_3 (the probability that my sense data are adequate and undistorted) x P_4 (the probability that my neural processing has made proper sense of the data) x P_5 (the probability that I have used appropriate patterns to understand the causal relations among the various forces and objects in view) x P_6 (etc., etc., etc.)...down to x

P_{large} (the probability that I've done all the foregoing estimating at least approximately correctly).

We would never do this, of course, nor could we if we would. This is just a thought experiment. The crucial questions we must consider are, How small will P get? and How will I behave in acknowledgement that P is always, always less than 1?

Nowhere in the hundreds of books that have been written on scientific method and the philosophy of science is there any rule suggested for recognizing the "true" theory, and it is the case that nobody knows how to do that. There are only guidelines for evaluating theories against the evidence and each other in order to decide which are more reasonable or useful. So science, our most powerful and successful tool for knowing, finds it cannot aspire to final truth and confesses, by its silence, that it wouldn't necessarily even recognize truth if bitten by it. Thus it must be for the rest of us. Our private search for knowledge can hardly hope to surpass scientific method in efficacy; why imagine that we could do better as to results?

The scientist follows procedures that keep reminding him of the provisional nature of his knowledge. He is constantly obliged to recall that he deals with hypotheses that are more or less probable, more or less well established, more or less useful, but not True Now And Forever.

> A philosopher once said "It is necessary for the very existence of science that the same conditions always produce the same results." Well, they do not....What is necessary "for the very existence of science," and what the characteristics of nature are, are not to be determined by pompous preconditions, they are determined always by the material with

which we work, by nature herself. We look,
and we see what we find, and we cannot say
ahead of time successfully what it is going to
look like. The most reasonable possibilities
often turn out not to be the situation. If
science is to progress, what we need is the
ability to experiment, honesty in reporting
results – the results must be reported
without somebody saying what they would
like the results to have been – and finally –
an important thing – the intelligence to
interpret the results. An important point
about this intelligence is that it should not be
sure ahead of time what must be....In fact it
is necessary for the very existence of science
that minds exist which do not allow that
nature must satisfy some preconceived
conditions, like those of our philosopher.
> –Richard Feynman

What would really be fair is if we all had some way of
reminding ourselves that this is the case for us, too.

The best we seem to be able to do along this line is to have
our wise persons issue from time to time a reminder of the
uncertain nature of knowledge and of the wisdom of
acknowledging our limitations.

When you know a thing, to hold that you
know it; and when you do not know a thing,
to allow that you do not know it – this is
knowledge.
> –Confucius

robert mchenry

Knowing what
thou knowest not
is in a sense
omniscience.

–Piet Hein

Conversation would be vastly improved by
the constant use of four simple words: I do
not know.

–André Maurois

Whatever inspiration is, it's born from a
continuous "I don't know." ...[K]nowledge
that doesn't lead to new questions quickly
dies out. It fails to maintain the temperature
required for sustaining life. In the most
extreme cases, well known from ancient and
modern history, it even poses a lethal threat
to society.

That is why I value that little phrase "I don't
know" so highly. It's small, but it flies on
mighty wings. It expands our lives to include
spaces within us as well as the outer
expanses in which our tiny Earth hangs
suspended. If Isaac Newton had never said
to himself "I don't know," the apples in his
little orchard might have dropped to the
ground like hailstones, and, at best, he
would have stooped to pick them up and
gobble them with gusto.

—Wislawa Szymborska

"Fifteen hundred years ago, everybody *knew*
the Earth was the center of the universe.
Five hundred years ago, everybody *knew* the

134

how to know

Earth was flat. And fifteen minutes ago you
knew that people were alone on this planet.
Imagine what you'll know tomorrow."
                    –Tommy Lee Jones

My personal motto is: "Strong opinions
weakly held."
                    –Paul Saffo

"I don't know" or "I cannot be certain" are simple enough
phrases, but they sometimes seem to unnerve us. We can
bring ourselves to pronounce them only with great difficulty.
Yet they are not only the truth, they are liberating and
empowering. They liberate us from the tyranny of comfortable
or simply familiar falsehood; they liberate us from the
irrational need to appear what we are not; and they empower
us to continue the search for knowledge and consequently to
know our world better.

("I don't know" can also be a very useful tool at a cocktail
party, should you happen to encounter one of those poor souls
whose motive for knowing is nothing more elevated than
combat and whose idea of knowing is trivial word associations.
"So, how about that War of Jenkins' Ear?" he challenges.
"Happen to recall what year that was?" You slowly allow a
quizzical expression onto your face and reply "I'm afraid I
haven't the least idea." If you do this just right, you can
almost see his crest fall as it dawns on him that you are
declining the contest not from ignorance but *de haut en bas*,
from above any such jejune pastime. This is a delectable
moment in itself, beyond the welcome fact that you now don't
have to match wits with this loser.)

Here is my own stab at a reminder, a mnemonic consisting of
three simple words: If you would know, you must do so

Courageously, Carefully, and Conditionally. Actually, that should be Courageously, Carefully, Conditionally, and Courageously Again, but we like things in threes. Let's look at each one.

courageously: It takes some courage to be prepared always to reexamine what we believe we know and to discard what no longer measures up to our highest standard, no matter how pleasant it may be to believe it and how easy it would be to continue to do so. To look a belief in the face and judge it fairly, no matter that you had it from your mother, or that your clan has always believed it, or that Jim Morrison said so, or that everybody knows it – that is courageous, and necessary. Put another way, knowing requires courage, not the courage to defend what we know or to impose it on others, but the courage to abandon it when it can no longer be defended.

carefully: Evaluating a candidate bit of knowledge against prior knowledge, experience, and consequences is prone to all the errors we have discussed. The results of the process will be no better than the care with which it is done. But be of good cheer. These are skills that can be learned, practiced, and (nearly) perfected. You merely have to desire to do so.

conditionally: "Conditionally" doesn't really mean exactly the same thing as "provisionally," but it's close and it does begin with "c". This is a marketing thing. You know what I mean.

courageously again: Even though we forever fall short of attaining certain or absolute knowledge, we are not thereby absolved from having to live and know responsibly. We cannot wait for what will not come; we are called on constantly to assess, to decide, to act, on the basis of incomplete and uncertain knowledge. Prudence will dictate that we proceed with all the care possible in each case and that, bearing in mind the provisional quality of what we are knowing, we remain alert to new information and indications of error; that we be prepared to shift base, cut losses, reassess, admit ignorance, all as required.

The final and most interesting lesson of the story of Croesus is just this. He took due care in qualifying Delphi as his source of knowledge, and having gotten and interpreted his answer, he acted courageously. In his case, it so befell that he had made an error of interpretation and his actions led to disaster.

That'll happen.

[1] Before commencing the writing of this book I made three resolutions. One, it would employ the fewest footnotes possible; this is it. Two, I would not retell yet again the ancient tale of the seven blind wise men and the elephant. (Specifically, I have omitted it from chapters 3 and 5.) Three, I would under no circumstances appeal to Gödel's Theorem to prove something.

postscript

For those few of you who didn't jump right up in the middle of Chapter 2 and run to Google the War of Jenkins' Ear, here's the story:

In the late 1730s the rivalry between England and Spain to dominate both the colonization of the Americas and the attending Atlantic trade produced a growing appetite for war. The British prime minister, Robert Walpole, was opposed to war but was growing old and losing command even of his own party. In 1738 one Captain Robert Jenkins appeared before a committee of the House of Commons and told of an attack on his ship by Spanish forces in the West Indies seven years earlier. In proof of his claim, he exhibited what he said was his own ear, sliced off, he said, by a Spaniard. This and other similar tales gave the war party all they needed to stir up public opinion. The war that commenced in October 1739 soon merged into the series of hostilities involving Britain, Spain, France, and Austria that is known collectively as the War of the Austrian Succession. Had enough?

Anyway, that's the story. No, really.

Printed in the United States
20117LVS00006B/433-456